Christine Penner Polle

UNFREEZE
YOURSELF

Five ways to take action on
climate change NOW
for the sake of your family,
your health, and the planet

outskirtspress
DENVER, COLORADO

Praise for *Unfreeze Yourself:*

"As parents, our love for our children is uncondi-tional; without thought, we regularly put their futures and their lives before ours. But too often the reality of climate change paralyses our actions, our hopes, our love and our future dreams for our children. With her wise counsel and supportive, practical simple plans of action, Christine helps us "unfreeze," reactivating our unconditional love. She reminds us why we can't fail, and with her guidance, we won't." Harriet Shugarman, Founder and Executive Director, ClimateMama

"*Unfreeze Yourself* is not just another book about how bad things are. Instead, it's a joyful, re-energizing read for busy people like you who don't want to be left out of a growing, life-giving movement of 'sacred activ-ism'. Being unfrozen feels so good, largely because it's about loving our children and grandchildren. Christine Penner Polle will help you find your own way there." Mardi Tindal, former Moderator of The United Church of Canada

"Christine Penner Polle has written a timely book to engage more people in the crucial issue of our time, global warming. Practical and encouraging, *Unfreeze Yourself* gives busy people ways to create a livable fu-ture that go beyond changing light bulbs and biking more. Do yourself and your grandchildren a favour and read this book – now!" Graham Saunders, author of

Gardening with Short Growing Seasons and President of Environment North, teaches and researches northern climate issues.

"In *Global Warming's Six Americas,* Anthony Lieserowitz identifies the largest group as people who are concerned but don't know what to do. Ms. Penner Polle lays out exactly what a person can do. The fact that she is a writer who has developed her craft makes *Unfreeze Yourself* both extremely useful and pleasant to read. For anyone who recognizes the scale of the problem we are dealing with in regards to global warming, this is an excellent primer to guide their particular response." Mark Reynolds, Executive Director, Citizens' Climate Lobby

"There is a paradigm shift coming and it's good news for us as individuals and the planet. If you want to know what that new world looks like and how we get there, read this book!" Shaun Loney, Ashoka Fellow and co-founder of 10 green economy social enterprises. He is an Ernst and Young Entrepreneur of the Year (2015) and author of *BUILD Prosperity: Energizing Manitoba's Local Economy.*

Outskirts Press, Inc.
http://www.outskirtspress.com

ISBN: 978-1-4787-5913-3

Outskirts Press and the "OP" logo are trademarks belonging to Outskirts Press, Inc.

PRINTED IN THE UNITED STATES OF AMERICA

*For my daughters Kate and Emma,
the reason I unfroze myself.*

Original artwork by Rebecca Saikkonen

Table of Contents

Introduction

The Climb-It Challenge

*Great things are done when men and mountains
meet; This is not done by jostling in the street.*

William Blake

Out for a family stroll recently, six-year old Gillian
surprised her mother with the pronouncement that
the reason her older brother hadn't attended a recent
march for climate action was because he wasn't a good
climber. It dawned on my friend that, for her daughter, climate change was "climb-it" change. The climate
awareness events this concerned mom had organized
had been, for Gillian, about people climbing stuff to
help the environment.

I laughed when I heard this story, but on reflection realized that Gillian's understanding of global warming
is spot-on. We *do* have a mountain in front of us that

needs climbing. The climate change mountain is blocking the road to a prosperous and happy future for all of us and our loved ones. The question is not *if* the mountain needs to be scaled, but rather *when* we will choose to tackle it. Every day of delay in lowering the carbon emissions that are overheating our atmosphere makes the mountain higher and the climb ahead more difficult.

There is no doubt that we live in a fast-paced and stressed-out world. There are many, often competing, demands on our time. Even if we hear the experts' warnings on the nightly news, it's hard to translate the implications of that science into every-day reality. Most of us are busier than ever, working flat out to keep a roof over our family's head, food on the table and, if we're lucky, set some money aside for our kids' college fund. We may be caring for aging parents. Our partners need loving attention. Perhaps we are wrestling with our own health concerns. At the end of the day, it often feels like we've climbed Mount Everest. Who has the time to scale another even more daunting peak? There is often no place and no energy left for the global ecological crisis scientists are warning us about.

Yet we know the storm clouds are gathering on the horizon. It is impossible to escape the reminders of environmental disaster. Interspersed between funny cat videos on Facebook are photos of rivers dying from agricultural runoff and oceans contaminated with oil. There are regular news reports of the changing jet stream and severe weather events linked to our overheated atmosphere. YouTube videos show tens of thousands of bats and whole flocks of birds dropping dead from the sky. Yet our hectic routines leave concerned people with little choice but to push worry about the state of the planet onto the back burner, to be attended to when and if we can find the time.

It's easy to push global climate change so far back that it falls off the stove completely. It's a huge, complex, and controversial issue. Though unchecked carbon emissions threaten our children's future health and safety, what can one person do? Climate change, or global warming (can't they just make up their minds what to call it?) is just too big a problem to think about, never mind act on.

But what if there was a way to ensure your loved ones had a livable world in the time it takes to attend one yoga class a week? What if acting on climate change improved your health as well as the health of the planet? What if acting to preserve a stable climate improved your family's quality of life in the present in addition to increasing your children's future health and happiness?

It is for busy but concerned people, particularly parents, that I wrote this book. As a mother of two who actively avoided the issue of climate change before becoming a climate advocate, I understand the demands on parents in this crazy time in which we're living. Having lived it, I know how strong the need is to look away from what is threatening our children's future. I wrote this book to share the *good* news from the climate front. Ensuring our children have a stable climate is not only great for the planet, it's good for your health and your family's well-being. As a bonus, it strengthens your community and even boosts your nation's economic prosperity. And – more good news - this work doesn't need to take any more time each week than watching two of your favourite TV shows.

There's no shortage of solutions for the climate crisis. What most people don't realize is that the only things missing to solve the climate crisis are political will and *you*. This book, rooted in experience, shows that facing the climate monster is less stressful than ignoring it.

I'm no stranger to worry and dread. A naturally fearful child, I spent many sleepless hours lying in bed waiting for the deadly pounce of monsters conjured by the nightly creaks and rattles of our old prairie farmhouse. One particular night was spent in heart-pounding, mouth-drying terror, anticipating the painful strike of the black snakes on my dresser. Imagine my relief when the morning sunshine revealed socks tossed carelessly away the night before.

Like the sun on those socks, this book shines a light on the climate change monster that is keeping so many of us frozen in despair and hopelessness. The relief that comes from facing our worst fears is exhilarating and liberating.

This book gives parents, grandparents, and everyone else practical steps to move from climate change avoidance and paralysis towards hopeful action. These strategies have a proven track record for making a difference. Along with practical tips, woven throughout the book is good news from around the world. Part two highlights the stories of people who have unfrozen themselves. They are beacons lighting the way to a post-carbon world. They demonstrate that there is an alternative to despair, and they offer hope. As author Rebecca Solnit reminds us, to hope is to commit yourself to the future and make the present inhabitable. Without hope, it is impossible to act.

> *Christine helped move me from paralyzed with fear about it to active engagement on climate change. I now feel hopeful and empowered, and who could have imagined it would be so much fun!*
>
> Valerie Blab, entrepreneur and mother of three, Ontario, Canada

There is a fork in the road ahead, and a choice to be made. Will you have to look your children in the eyes down the road and apologize to them for not acting while there was still time? Or will your children and grandchildren thank you for speaking up for their future? Which legacy will you choose? This incredible moment offers each of us an opportunity to reclaim the climate, the economy, and our democracy for future generations. History, author Naomi Klein reminds us, is knocking on our door.

The information and practical steps you are about to read will reduce anxiety and unleash creativity and passion just when the world needs it most. If you want new tools to help you move from hopelessness to empowerment, keep reading. Each chapter provides insight and practical steps to take to create the future we all want, one that contains a livable world for our children.

The global warming mountain is a challenge that *can* be conquered. Adventurers who climb difficult peaks say that mountains are not only invitations to ascend to new heights; they also call us to become better versions of ourselves. Getting to a peak requires effort but once you reach the summit, the glorious new world before you is well worth it.

The longest journey, we are told, starts with a single step. It's time to begin.

> *Today is your day! Your mountain is waiting, so... get on your way!*
>
> Dr. Seuss

PART I
Unfreezing

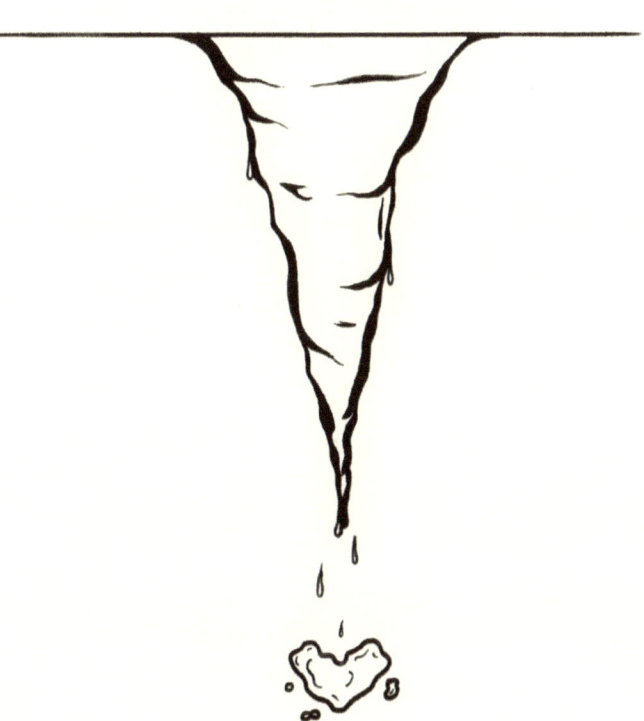

CHAPTER 1

Hope is a Verb: My Story

hope
verb|hōp
to want something to happen or be true and think that it could happen or be true

Hope is a verb with its sleeves rolled up.

Dr. David Orr

"There's nothing we can do about global warming that would make a difference," new mom Sally told me with a hopeless shrug.

It was a beautiful summer day. My husband and I sat on our back deck with our friends we'll call Sally and

Dale. They had dropped in to introduce us to their new daughter Nina. For months before Nina's arrival, the excited parents had been getting ready for the birth of their much-anticipated first child. Part of their preparation involved countless hours of research on the risks of environmental toxins to children, and how to avoid them. These new parents, like most, were working hard to safeguard their precious little one. They spared no expense to protect her from man-made hazards. By the time Nina arrived, her pink and yellow nursery had nontoxic paint on its walls, and organic cotton was the sole fabric that touched Nina's delicate skin. When solid food was added to her diet of breast milk, the homemade, all-organic baby food was stored in stainless steel containers so no BPA contamination reached her growing body.

As we sat on our deck cooing at the baby and catching up on our lives, the conversation veered towards the problem of climate change. All of us agreed it was a serious threat to our children's future safety. Yet when we invited the new parents to join our recently formed Citizens' Climate Lobby group and be part of working for change, they declined. Despite knowing the risky future ahead for Nina and her peers because of our unchecked carbon emissions, these intelligent and informed young parents couldn't be moved into action. They felt overwhelmed by the challenge of global warming.

They are not alone. I have seen the same hopelessness in a young mom with tears streaming down her face while we chatted at a neighbourhood park. She pushed her chubby-cheeked toddler in the swing while she shared that she had spent much of her just-completed maternity leave crying. She couldn't stop contemplating the devastated planet her son was going to inherit. At a farmer's market recently, a business man haltingly told me of his grief at the future his sons were going to face with a destabilized climate.

Every parent knows that their number one duty is to protect their children. But in an age of global climate change there is an undercurrent of despair beneath the frenetic busyness that is parenting in the 21st Century. I've heard from anguished yet paralyzed people again and again in my years as a climate-concerned parent and activist. I've seen the same haunted expression on the faces of mothers and fathers, young people and grandparents, all across Canada, as they tell me there's nothing they can do to change the disastrous course we are on. Climate trauma is real and many of us are suffering from it. Psychiatrist Dr. Lise Van Susteren calls this emotional reaction to the reality of a climate-changed world "pre-traumatic stress disorder." It describes the mental anguish that results from preparing for the worst, before it actually happens.

The pages that follow are a response to all the Sallys and Dales out there. It's written for parents who love their children and this beautiful world, but who can't see a way out of hopelessness and paralysis. There *are* solutions for the problem of global warming and each of us can take practical steps to ensure that these solutions become reality.

Climate change, with all that it symbolizes about our unsustainable way of life in this industrial age, is the challenge of our time. We are not unique in facing difficult times, though. Other generations had different challenges that only seem less daunting to us in hindsight. The "Greatest Generation" fought against overwhelming odds in World War II against the Nazi threat. Millions paid the ultimate price to make the world safe from fascism for future generations. The U.S. civil rights movement waged a long battle for the equality of all people under the law. This struggle sometimes made activists the targets of violence and pitted them against law enforcement. Centuries ago abolitionists challenged an entire economy run on the "dirty energy" of slaves. Persistence and a commitment to a vision of a better world were essential to the success of all of these crusades.

Looking back on history, we can see a pattern: again and again, people who weren't deterred by the impossible overcame seemingly insurmountable challenges. Just because climate change seems hopeless doesn't mean it is. With no guarantee of success, our forefathers and mothers forged ahead in difficult times. In doing so, they changed the world for the better. Who are we, then, to say the impossible can't be done?

It only seems impossible until it's done.

Nelson Mandela

Beyond Paralysis

Let's agree that life isn't fair. Given other options, perhaps we wouldn't have chosen this particular time in Earth's history to be alive. Now might be a good time to shout "Life Sucks!" as many times as you need to, or pound your pillow; whatever is required to transition from resentment to acceptance. Like it or not, climate change is *our* challenge. There is good news, though. At times of great danger there is also great possibility. We have the incredible opportunity to use this crisis to make our children's lives safer, healthier, and more prosperous. As I write this, there is still a window open for us to act to save much of the world for future generations.

The good news: The changes we must make to avoid ultimate collapse are identical to the changes we must make to create the world of our common dream.

David Korten

The benefits of action extend beyond creating a better world. Acting to create a livable future makes as much a difference for us as it does for our children. That's a bold statement but one I'm willing to repeat: *working to create a safe world for future generations gives as much to us as it gives to them*. Most people, as Henry David Thoreau pointed out, lead lives of quiet desperation. Often we fear to venture far beyond our comfort zone unless we are pushed. The huge scale of the climate crisis requires us all to move into uncharted territory.

My Own Inconvenient Truth

I can speak with confidence on this topic because I speak from personal experience. Climate trauma is not just a theoretical construct for me, I have lived it. I spent years turning off the television or radio if climate change was up next. I never found a convenient time to watch *An Inconvenient Truth*. I knew the news was bad for the planet and, by implication and much closer to home, for my two daughters who were born in the early 1990s.

Like other baby boomers, I came of age under the shadow of the Cold War and the spectre of nuclear holocaust. Nine months after I arrived on this planet, Cuban President Osvaldo Dorticós stood in front of the UN General Assembly to say, "If...we are attacked, we will defend ourselves. I repeat, we have suffi-cient means with which to defend ourselves." Before

I turned 10 months old, the world had come as close to full-scale nuclear war as it ever would during the Cold War, as the United States and the U.S.S.R played a grim game of chicken over nuclear missiles placed on Cuban soil.

While in university in the 1980s, I signed petitions against the U.S. involvement in Nicaragua and marched in the annual Peace March. Mostly, though, I just worried about what the future held. In case nuclear annihilation wasn't enough to keep a young person up at night, this was also when scientists discovered that industrial pollution was making the rain falling from the sky acidic enough to kill maple trees and lakes in Quebec and Maine. And, to add to the nightmare-inducing list, people were cautioned to slip on a t-shirt, slap on a hat, and slop on sunscreen because the protective ozone layer was disappearing above our heads thanks to man-made aerosols.

Then everything seemed to change. I was pregnant with my first daughter when the Berlin Wall fell as Glasnost flooded the Soviet Union and signalled the beginning of the end of the Cold War. 1989 also marked the start of the implementation of the Montreal Protocol, the international treaty negotiated two years earlier to phase out the use of ozone-depleting chemicals. A banner year, 1989 was also the year that the U.S. Congress passed a series of amendments to the Clean Air Act including "The Acid Rain Program" that instituted a cap and trade system to control the factory emissions that were blighting trees and lakes in northeastern North America.

All this progress towards peace and a cleaner environment was enough to make a new mom relax. The lesson I took from these changes was that there were people who were much more important, informed, and well-placed than me who were working on the problems that had caused me so much anxiety. And, unlike my peace marches and petitions, these people were able to impact events and improve the state of the world. Some cautious optimism snuck into my worldview; while world leaders and our industrial economy had led us to the edge of some nasty precipices, sanity had prevailed in the end.

But it turns out there wasn't much respite for a worried parent. Unbeknownst to me, in June 1988 Dr. James Hansen, climatologist and head of NASA's Goddard Institute for Space Studies, testified in front of the U.S. Senate Energy and Natural Resources Committee that the recent planet-wide warming trend was caused by a buildup of carbon dioxide and other artificial gases in the atmosphere. The *New York Times* headline read *"Global Warming Has Begun, Expert Tells Senate"*.

In November 1988 the Intergovernmental Panel on Climate Change (IPCC) was formed in Geneva Switzerland to provide policy makers around the globe with a clear scientific view on climate change and its potential environmental and socio-economic impacts.

In 1990, two weeks after my daughter Kate turned six months old, Conservative British Prime Minister Margaret Thatcher gave a speech to the 2nd World Climate Conference where she said:

> Mr. Chairman, since the last World War, our world has faced many challenges, none more vital than that of defending our liberty and keeping the peace.

> ...But the threat to our world comes not only from tyrants and their tanks. It can be more insidious though less visible. The danger of global warming is as yet unseen, but real enough for us to make changes and sacrifices, so that we do not live at the expense of future generations.

> Our ability to come together to stop or limit damage to the world's environment will be perhaps the greatest test of how far we can act as a world community. No-one should underestimate the imagination that will be required, nor the scientific effort, nor the unprecedented co-operation we shall have to show. We shall need statesmanship of a rare order. It's because we know that, that we are here today.

Despite the global alarm bells, it took me almost two decades after this dramatic speech to allow the severity of the climate crisis to filter into my consciousness. No parent with young children needs an explanation of how busy our family's life was. This was especially true once I became the main bread winner during the eight years my husband was in school. Like every parent who works, my hands were full. When not at work I was occupied with the demands of nourishing my daughters' minds and bodies while being married to a busy medical student.

But it was more than our family's hectic schedule that kept me from becoming more informed about the threat of global warming. I could, and did, alter my shopping habits after learning about the sweatshops where underpaid employees worked in deplorable conditions to churn out cheap clothes for the North American market. I also switched to fair trade organic chocolate (because who can give it up completely?) after hearing about child slavery and pesticide use on cocoa plantations. But what on Earth could I do that would make an impact on a problem as big as climate change? As a family, we were already using compact fluorescent light bulbs. We walked and biked and used public transport as much as we could. We even grew some of our own food, although that was sheer good fortune, as I'm lucky to be married to an avid gardener.

I didn't consciously make the decision to stay uninformed and uninvolved. But looking back it's clear I felt that I couldn't make a difference on an issue of such global proportions. And in my defense, the international community had been effective in decreasing the threat of nuclear war and managing the twin environmental challenges of ozone depletion and acid rain. There was some reason to hope that climate change would also be solved at that level. As Prime Minister Thatcher said, statesmen and women were needed to solve this problem and I knew I wasn't one of those.

But the alarm bells didn't go away, they got louder. Just before Halloween 2005, Leonardo DiCaprio told Oprah's audience that global warming was not only the number one issue affecting the environment, it was one of the most important issues facing all of humanity.

One year later, the film *An Inconvenient Truth* about Al Gore's tireless campaign to educate citizens about global warming won several Academy Awards. The movie's message was clear: humans are causing global warming, and its effects are already devastating.

It was becoming harder to ignore both the threat of global warming and the lack of international action on it, but I, and millions of busy parents like me, did just that. Unfortunately politicians increasingly began to take their cues more from preoccupied voters than from scientists. Global action on lowering our climate-destabilizing emissions stalled, after having begun so promisingly with the formation of the IPCC and with the signing of the world's first international climate treaty (the Kyoto Accord) in 1992.

It wasn't until 2009 that a series of events put global climate change front and centre in my awareness. A writing contract required me to immerse myself in research about current environmental issues, including climate change. At the same time I read *Geography of Hope* by Canadian author Chris Turner. Prompted by the birth of his daughter and his contemplation of the grim future that might await her if we don't change our unsustainable ways, Turner scoured the globe for signs of hope. His book shines a light on people and communities around the world that are creatively and optimistically taking on environmental challenges.

The concerns that my research had raised intensified during the summer of 2009. It was a season of unpredictable and unseasonably cool weather in northern Ontario. For the first time in my life I checked the weather forecast daily, sometimes hourly, wondering when summer was finally going to arrive. Thus I was a receptive audience when an email showed up in my inbox that introduced a new organization called 350.org that was focused on creating a global climate movement. 350.org's website described global warming in a way I could understand: a concentration below 350 parts per million (ppm) of carbon dioxide (CO_2) in the atmosphere is what science tells us is required to maintain a livable planet for humans. The carbon dioxide level in our atmosphere is now higher than that, and is rising steadily as we keep burning fossil fuels. In September, 2009, when I first visited 350.org's website the global carbon dioxide level sat at around 387 parts per million. As I write this in early spring 2015 the global CO_2 level, measured at Mauna Loa Observatory in Hawaii since the 1950s, is 400.26.

350.org's website stated it succinctly:

> Two years ago, after leading climatologists observed rapid ice melt in the Arctic and other frightening signs of climate change, they issued a series of studies showing that the planet faced both human and natural disaster if atmospheric concentrations of CO_2 remained above 350 parts per million.

Hope as a Verb

In October 2009, I couldn't go back to my state of not-so-blissful ignorance about the climate crisis, even if I'd wanted to. After organizing a small event in my community for 350.org's International Day of Climate Action, I felt compelled to do more. But what could a not-very-politically-active, climate-concerned mom from northern Ontario, Canada do that would make a difference?

> You do not measure the fruit of your action. You have to measure your obligation to action.

Dr. Vandana Shiva, physicist and food activist

I felt a moral obligation to act, as a mother, a person of faith, and someone who had benefited greatly from being born in a rich nation. I didn't know if my actions would make a difference but I moved ahead despite my insecurities. The certainty of success wasn't as important as being able to tell my children some day that I had done everything that I could. Writing and research was something I knew how to do, so I started there. I borrowed *Blogging for Dummies* from the library and on Halloween Day 2009 I launched my blog *350orbust.com*.

The posts on my blog reflect my state of mind during those early years as a climate activist. I express anger, frustration and fear as international climate talks failed, media-savvy climate deniers twisted the scientific facts, and my federal government's commitment to emission cuts dwindled. There are five stages of grief: denial, anger, bargaining, depression, and acceptance. Having passed through the denial phase I spent much of the next three years in anger and depression. Although fear isn't listed in the traditional grief stages, I would argue that it is the root of all of the stages except the final one. Underneath the anger I expressed on my blog was enormous, almost paralyzing, fear. There is much to fear when looking the global warming monster in the face. Unchecked climate change will make our children and grandchildren's world inhospitable and, eventually, uninhabitable.

Here we are in 2015, six years after my conversion from climate change avoider to climate-concerned parent and lobbyist. Experts are increasingly alarmed about the global inaction on emissions reduction. Canada has withdrawn from the ultimately ineffectual Kyoto Protocol and no international climate treaty has taken its place. Industrialized countries continue to argue over climate compensation funds with island nations that are drowning as sea levels rise. China and India's emissions grow daily. Global carbon dioxide levels have spent more and more time above 400 parts per million, and are expected to be permanently above 400 ppm within a few years. Extreme drought and wildfires in western North America dominate news headlines. As I write this we are only halfway through 2015 but the year is on track to be the hottest year in the record books. There continues to be little coverage of the climate crisis in the mainstream media. When a climate story is aired, more often than not PR-trained but unscientific climate deniers are given equal time with scientists who have spent years studying this problem. Yet this book is about moving out of the frozen fear state and taking action. If the news is getting worse, how is that possible?

If you have read this far, you are already aware that there is an urgent problem with the way humans are using up the Earth's finite resources. You know that our current way of life isn't sustainable. At the end of this book, Appendix One (*Where are we going and why are we in this handbasket?*) summarizes what the science says about global warming, ocean acidification, and biodiversity loss. Feel free to use it as a resource.

In the meantime, let's dive into practical and attainable steps for you to take. The fact is that the climate crisis gives us the opportunity to create a *better* future for generations to come. If we roll up our sleeves and make hope a verb, not just a dream, the coming shift will be an extraordinary time when ordinary people will accomplish tremendous things. To get started down a new path, it's helpful to have a map to follow. The coming chapters are such a guide. Some of the actions offered may appeal more than others; take note of the ones that resonate with you, even (or especially) if they are outside your comfort zone. The world doesn't need more people acting out of fear or obligation. Now more than ever the world needs people doing things that light them, and the world, up.

> *We are an extraordinary species, and we are capable of great things. History is full of evidence that when our backs are against the wall, all the great qualities of humanity, our compassion, our drive, our technical brilliance, and our ability to make things happen on a massive global scale, come strongly to the fore.*
>
> Paul Gilding, *The Great Disruption*

Talk Therapy: *Changing the Climate Conversation*

Climate change isn't the elephant in the room; it's the elephant we're all inside of.

Veteran ABC journalist Bill Blakemore

I am not naturally extroverted. In the first few years after I came out of the closet as a climate-concerned mom and blogger, I had to summon courage to bring climate change into casual conversations and especially more public discussions. It got easier as time went on, as my alarm about the unfolding global catastrophe eclipsed my concern of what people would think of me. I joked that bringing up climate change felt as socially awkward as public flatulence. It often provoked the same reaction; people were embarrassed, looked away, changed the subject and/or pretended not to hear.

It wasn't until I read George Marshall's book *Don't Even Think About It: Why Our Brains Are Wired to Ignore Climate Change* that I found an explanation for this phenomenon. As Marshall explains:

> *Really, though, it doesn't seem to matter how I say [climate change], because the result is almost always the same: The words collapse, sink, and die in midair, and the conversation suddenly changes course. It is like an invisible force field that you discover only when you barge right into it. Few people go that far, because, without ever having been told, they have somehow learned that this topic is out-of-bounds. That is why they know if someone else inadvertently enters the zone, it is a good idea to find something new to talk about.*

This silence about climate change is what is called a "meta-silence;" a silence about our silence on this issue.

> *The meta-silence is that we don't talk about the elephant in the room, and we don't talk about the fact that we don't talk about it.*

Professor Eviatar Zerubavel

Ironically, this allows the elephant to get bigger and bigger. In the case of climate change, it allows governments to put off action on emissions reduction and the shift to a clean energy economy while bringing the global climate closer to a dangerous tipping point.

Naming the Elephant

The first step in taking action on climate change is a deceptively simple one: commit to talking about climate change with one new person every day. It's deceptive because once you decide to do this, you will find yourself in situations where you will be forced to choose between embarrassment and your commitment to your children's future. Humans are hardwired to avoid humiliation; there's a reason why it's called "dying" of embarrassment. While there are important social functions that embarrassment plays, in the case of climate change it is dangerous to allow our fear of breaking the meta-silence have the upper hand. Nobody has ever actually died of embarrassment; on the other hand, fossil fuel pollution and extreme weather events cause more and more deaths every year.

When you deliberately speak out, you break the climate silence that has allowed governments to ignore this looming crisis for decades. You are being the change that is needed in the world right now; YOU are a climate champion.

> *I made a decision that fundamentally changed my life...I decided the survival of life on planet Earth mattered more to me than any discouragement, fear, or self-invalidation I might carry.*

Madeline Para, Program Director, Citizens' Climate Lobby

Dancing With the Elephant

As I and the other organizers were preparing for a panel discussion about climate change that was being held at a local university, an audience member brought up a pamphlet that had been distributed on each seat. We were horrified. The pamphlet was a two-page rant about the death and destruction about to be rained down on the earth and humanity because of global warming. No solutions were offered, just a shopping list of horrors. The pamphlet was a textbook example of how *not* to communicate about climate change.

Nobody wants to spend time with a zealot, so here are some pointers to help you bring up climate change without coming across as one of those. To do your part to avoid uncomfortable conversations, this chapter offers some suggestions on how to dance delicately with the climate elephant. It's a challenging but not impossible feat.

The goal is to drop the "cc" term into a conversation and offer the other person a chance to respond. It is *not* to corner an innocent bystander and pour out all your accumulated information on, and angst about, global warming.

It is not easy to dance elegantly with the climate change elephant. Here are some tips to help keep your dance card full (and the room from emptying):

- **Use the "I" word.** It is difficult to argue with a statement from your personal perspective, especially if you use the words, "I feel..." Share your personal concern about this global issue. For example, "I'm worried about the impact of more extreme weather events on my nieces and nephews" or, "As a Christian/Muslim/Jew/Buddhist/etc, it keeps me up at night thinking about the fact that the poorest people are paying the price for our country's continued use of fossil fuels."

- **Connect climate change to current issues.** Naturally work it into the conversation. Don't try too hard; this is a marathon we are on, not a sprint. As climate change's impacts become increasingly widespread and frequent, it becomes easier and easier to link it to the latest news headlines.

David Rifka volunteers for Citizen's Climate Lobby and blogs at *flyingwithgeese.com*. In a blog post entitled "Climate's not really my thing" Rivka shares some advice about broaching the topic of global warming:

> My friend Liza says engaging people in a conversation about climate is like the California drought. The ground is so parched, the only way it can take in water, is slowly, slowly, slowly, over time. The ground needs to soften before it can even begin to absorb anything. The predicted El Nino storms will not reverse the drought. They might even make things worse. Most of the water will flood backyards and streets and run off into storm drains.
>
> Liza says we can't deluge people with information. First soften the ground. If I am like El Nino, raining down buckets of information, my words will run off into the storm drain. Slowly, slowly, slowly soften the ground.

Rifka's friend Liza offers excellent advice. When it comes to changing the climate conversation, let's be a soft and steady rain that refreshes and nourishes, not a deluge or a drought.

- **Avoid easy labels.** Like it or not, environmentalists have a bad reputation in some quarters these days. If you lead with, "I'm concerned about climate change because I'm an environmentalist," you may lose the person you're reaching out to before they hear all the great things you have to say. Rather than taking that chance, even if you proudly wear the environmentalist label, consider other ways of identifying yourself that are equally true and perhaps easier to relate to. Because climate change affects my children and future generations, I often describe myself as a climate-concerned mom. Are you a farmer? A gardener? A fisherman or woman? A health care professional? A small business owner? These are all ways to start a conversation about climate change; be creative!

Peterson Tuscano, a volunteer for Citizens' Climate Lobby who blogs at ClimateStew.com, suggests starting a conversation with, "I am not an environmentalist but I am concerned about climate change." If you are an environmentalist Tuscano recommends, "Sure I'm an environmentalist but I don't see climate change as simply an environmental issue."

One of my fellow Citizens' Climate Lobby volunteers, or CCLer, is an entrepreneur and has sold Mary Kay cosmetics for years. She often introduces herself as someone who sells lipstick, which disarms people. As a consequence, she has reached people who would never listen to a typical "treehugger."

- **Focus on values.** While global warming is a planetary issue, what most people care about is much more local. The challenge of communicating about it is to make those close-to-home connections. You're well on the way if you've opened up the conversation by leading with the reasons you are concerned about climate change. The natural next step is to connect on the values that you share with the person or people with whom you are speaking. This is where it helps to know your audience. What do they hold dear? Is it family, community, care for creation, the economy, national security, or the common good? Everyone, even those with whom we disagree politically, will value one or more of these. It's your job to figure out which ones hold the most sway with your audience, and to connect climate change to one or more of them. There is a strong case to be made that delaying action on climate change will have a negative impact on all of these things.

We care about climate change because it is making our water more scarce here in west Texas where we live; because it impacts our local economy; because it affects our kids' health and their future security; and because our faith commands us to love and care for others, especially those who lack the resources we do. We all have the values we need to care about climate change; we just need to make the connection.

Dr Katharine Hayhoe, *Talking Climate*

A great example of this approach happened when my fellow climate lobbyist (Valerie the lipstick saleswoman) and I went door knocking last September. We hadn't traveled to New York for The People's Climate March but we wanted to do our part to raise awareness. As we approached one home, we could see the owner, whom we'll call Fred, in the garage busily stacking wood for winter. It became clear that Fred wasn't enthusiastic about having his day interrupted. When asked if he was concerned about climate change, Fred barked back at us that yes he was concerned but we were all hypocrites; we all drove cars and he, like most of his friends, didn't want to give up his fishing boat. It would have been easy to be put off by his gruffness and move on, but Val and I are made of sterner stuff. A shared value – we were all concerned about climate change – had been established. Asked whether he would like to have the option of choosing a less climate-polluting car or boat, Fred agreed. When the discussion shifted to solutions like putting a price on carbon and returning the money to citizens to make the move to a clean energy economy, the three of us agreed on that, too. In fairly short order, a conversation that started off as an argument was transformed. Fred signed our petition and we moved on before he put us to work stacking firewood.

- **Don't argue about the science.** Unless you are a climate scientist, debating the science of climate change is counter-productive. What we non-scientists can affirm is that 97 percent of climate scientists are convinced, based on the evidence, that human-caused global warming is happening. The majority of people are *very* concerned about climate change, and vastly outnumber those who deny the scientific consensus. It is possible that you could end up bumping into one of the minority (I know I have). If the person you are speaking with insists on discussing the scientific validity of global warming, politely change the subject and move on.

It can be helpful to share one or two facts, without using scientific jargon, from a source that your audience trusts. Sometimes it's best if the source isn't Al Gore, who has become, for some on the political right, a distrusted symbol of environmental hypocrisy. It could be someone like the President of the World Bank, Jim Yong Kim, or Pope Francis. Both of these men have been outspoken about the need to take action on climate change. Or perhaps the person you're engaging with isn't aware that the insurance industry is raising the alarm over the rise in extreme weather events across the globe. The increasingly acidic ocean, the overheated atmosphere's marine counterpart, may be a less controversial topic. Many people who vaguely distrust atmospheric climate science know nothing about the supporting evidence offered by a warming and increasingly acid ocean.

Simple messages, repeated often, by trusted messengers are powerful...be consistent, and don't be afraid of repeating critical points.

ecoAmerica, *Communicating on Climate*

- **Focus on solutions.** What is lacking is *not* solutions to the climate crisis but the political will to tackle the problem. There is more in-depth discussion about solutions, including putting a price on carbon, in Chapter Six.

A key communication point is that there is hope even at this late stage. It's also helpful to underscore the potential we have for building a better world as we respond to the challenges of global warming. Emphasizing that other generations have risen to the obstacles placed in their path, and that we can as well, offers an inspiring perspective.

> *It is true that the crisis coming will almost certainly see great conflict among nations over resources and refugees, mass suffering, and some difficult situations emerge as fear and nationalism rear their ugly heads. We need to plan for all of this. However, we will also see the best humanity can offer: great compassion, extraordinary innovation, and millions of people digging deep and finding their capacity for brilliance and innovation. This is because scientists, researchers, business leaders, community organizers, policy makers, entrepreneurs, and youth are all out there now, building the future we need. They just need our permission and support to take their work to mass scale.*

Paul Gilding, *The Great Disruption*

- **Don't be discouraged** if the person you are speaking with chooses not to take the opportunity to engage in the discussion that you are offering. Focus on the fact that you found the courage to bring climate change into the conversation. The next person, or perhaps the 20th person, that you speak with could be the one who has been lying awake at night worrying about the planet's future. You will offer them hope, like water given to a person dying of thirst. In addition, you never know what seed you may have planted in the seemingly uninterested person.

- **Persevere.** New research is showing that grit, or stick-to-itiveness, is essential for success in life.

Grit, it appears, is as important as intelligence or talent for overcoming life's challenges. Grit is an essential trait for climate champions. Those of us speaking up for a stable climate need to dig deep into our stores of grit. Like world-changers before us, we need to be committed to this issue for as long as it takes to achieve our goal.

Grit is passion and perseverance for very long term goals. Grit is stamina. Living life like it's a marathon and not a sprint.

Dr. Angela Duckworth, *The Key To Success? Grit*

Time for Change Action Step

Talk about climate change every day. With different people. Including elected officials.

Here are some tips to make this happen:

1. Make a list of the five people you are going to talk to about climate change in the next week. Beside each name, note how you are going to approach them. Are you going to call them on the phone? Bring it up at lunch break at the office? Talk to the person beside you on the bus? Once you've got a plan for each person written down, put the list in a place where you'll see it every day, like your fridge or beside your bed. When you've talked to them, place a checkmark beside their name. If you had an

unexpected conversation with someone, add their name, along with a big checkmark, to your list.

2. Once you've talked to these five people, add five new people to your list. And so on.

3. Once you have some practice starting up climate change conversations with neighbours and friends, it's time to talk to decision-makers. If you don't already know, look up who represents you at the local, provincial or state, and federal level. Write down their names in the order you are going to contact them.

While speaking with politicians may seem daunting, don't let anxiety stop you. I remember how nervous I was the first time I dialed up my Member of Parliament. I was 47 years old and had never in my life contacted an MP about any issue. I felt intimidated. If you feel the same way, you could begin by hand writing a letter (*not* sending an email or a computer-generated letter. See Omar Ahmad's TED Talk on "Political change with a pen and paper" for more on this). Two weeks later, you can follow up your letter with a call to the politician's office if you haven't heard back from them.

Whether you are writing or telephoning, it's important to keep the tone polite, brief, and focused on a single message. Always start a letter or conversation with an expression of appreciation for something the official has done. Be sure to mention solutions to our climate conundrum (solutions are discussed in detail in Chapter Six). Don't forget to thank them at the end, and let them know you will be communicating with them in the future

In Canada, letters to MPs in Ottawa don't require postage. In the United States, letters to Congressional representatives require a regular stamp.

As a person who now meets regularly with elected officials, from town councillors to members of the provincial parliament to federal Members of Parliament, I can't emphasize enough how important it is to tell elected officials that you are concerned about global warming. In meeting after meeting, I've heard politicians say that they've never, or rarely, heard from a constituent who is concerned about climate change. If you are concerned about climate change and haven't spoken to your elected representatives, is it any wonder that there is no political will for change? Politicians take action when they hear from the people who elect them.

4. Don't forget to congratulate yourself for every climate discussion you have. Keep your list of names updated, including the checkmarks after you've reached out to someone (maybe two for contacting an elected official!). This will track your progress.

> With each conversation, you are becoming a climate champion.

If you commit to shifting the climate conversation by speaking to one new person every day about it, how much time will this take out of your busy schedule? A very generous time allocation is five minutes each day multiplied by seven days. That's 35 minutes each week. Most weeks this action will take considerably less time, for several reasons. First, many people won't be interested in discussing climate change, so chances are the majority of conversations will be significantly shorter than five minutes. The second reason is that, with a bit of practice, you will begin to weave climate change seamlessly into interactions that already are part of your day. You will become a climate champion as you go about your daily routine.

Ripples of Hope

Rome wasn't built in a day, and the climate conversation won't be changed overnight either. Don't wait - start right away! Know that by talking to people in your circle of influence, you are sending out ripples that will continue far beyond. Your courage and persistence will end up inspiring more people than you will ever know.

> *Each time a [wo]man stands up for an ideal, or acts to improve the lot of others, or strikes out against injustice [s]he sends forth a tiny ripple of*

hope, and those ripples build a current which can sweep down the mightiest walls of oppression and resistance.

Senator Robert Kennedy

Good News for a Change

"The beginning of the end of fossil fuels" announced headlines in April, 2015. The question has become not if but when the world will be fueled entirely by clean energy. Bloomberg Business declared that the turning point in the shift to renewable energy actually happened two years earlier. In 2013 the world added 143 gigawatts of renewable electricity capacity, as opposed to just 141 gigawatts of fossil fuel capacity. Globally, more renewable power is being added each year than coal, natural gas, and oil combined. "The electricity system is shifting to clean," stated Michael Liebreich of the Bloomberg New Energy Foundation.

The shift to a clean energy economy has happened, and will continue to accelerate. There's no going back now.

CHAPTER 3

Group Therapy:
Connecting With Others

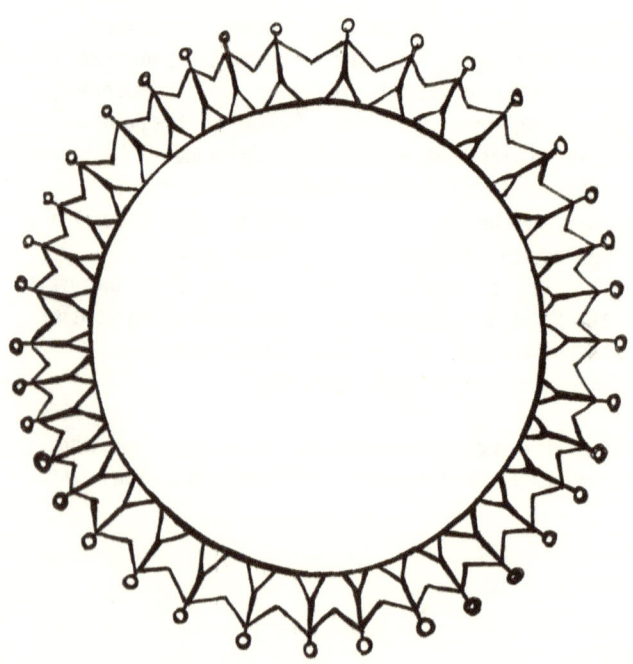

*Climate change is way too important
an issue to take on alone.*

Mark Reynolds, Executive Director,
Citizens' Climate Lobby

The common wisdom that there is strength in numbers definitely applies if you are concerned about global warming. After my global warming epiphany in 2009, I searched eagerly for other equally concerned folks to connect with, both online and in person. Being a newbie to the climate change arena, I wanted to learn from more experienced activists. I also wanted to offer my time and energy, of which I had more than experience. Linking up with other people passionate about this issue was much, much harder than I originally imagined. Luckily for me, I discovered Facebook at that time, to my teenage daughters' chagrin, and scoured its pages for climate groups that might offer inspiration and community. I travelled halfway across the country to meet up with other climate-concerned Canadians at a conference in Toronto in 2010. The connections that I made provided me with encouragement and the foundation for a community that I sorely needed. Eventually those connections resulted in me joining a newly formed climate organization, Citizens' Climate Lobby (CCL). Without persistence and some good luck, however, I would have been left feeling isolated, alone, and discouraged.

Engaging Head, Heart, and Feet

We human beings are moved to get involved in an issue or an organization when it touches us at an emotional level as well as an intellectual one. There is a reason that, in the summer of 2015, the tragic image of a toddler's body washed up on a Turkish beach galvanized the world about the Syrian refugee crisis that had been going on for years and had left many others dead. The heartbreaking photo of little Aylan touched people's hearts and millions of people around the world responded with action.

To act on climate, we need to have our head *and* hearts engaged. Canadian author and long-time environmentalist Liz Armstrong describes how this happened to her during a CCL conference in 2013:

> *I have known about the potentially catastrophic effects of climate change since the late 1980s, when I listened to the five-part CBC Radio series about the environment called It's A Matter of Survival. Somehow, all of the other issues that David Suzuki raised during that series seemed fairly easily 'fixable' by comparison – toxic chemicals in our environment, the mountains of garbage we industrialized humans create, and so on. But climate change? Because the consequences of burning fossil fuels present themselves as a 'slow emergency' given the decades-long time lag between the cause*

and effect of dumping vast quantities of CO_2 into our atmosphere, plus our delirious love affair with - and utter dependence on - fossil fuels, I came away from that climate episode knowing this was 'The Big One.' Over the years, it was − frankly − agony knowing this problem was relentlessly unfolding, yet so little was being accomplished to fight it given the massive pushback from all the fossil fuel interests profiting so enormously from their climate-warming pollution.

I did what I could - local education with kids and adults, made donations to climate change-oriented groups like the Suzuki Foundation and 350.org − but it all seemed so ineffective. It wasn't until I heard about the Citizens' Climate Lobby in Summer 2013 that I really thought: 'Hey, here's a group that seems focused, has resources, and can empower people like me to do something concrete to push for change where it counts − with governments and policymakers!' So I decided at the last minute to go to CCL Canada's first national conference in Ottawa in late November. I am not normally a big fan of conferences - too much sitting, too many (often boring!) speakers, etc. What a great surprise to meet both the US and Canadian founders of the organization - all humble, passionate, knowl-edgeable people − and to hear some very good presentations by excellent speakers. But the most profound part of all, for me, was to be emotionally

*touched by so many great people in this group,
because when my heart is engaged, it's way, WAY
easier for me to get my head and feet going too.*

Bingo, with CCL, I was "home."

The rest of this chapter discusses ways that you, like
Liz, can find your climate home.

The Right Recipe

Happily, as the movement to preserve a stable climate
grows, it's easier to find other concerned people. The
climate movement is growing by leaps and bounds,
while most of us are more connected than ever via social media. If you are one of those people who doesn't
consider yourself a "joiner," please reconsider that approach on the issue of climate change. As the quote
at the beginning of the chapter says, this is just too big
and important an issue to take on alone. The support
and companionship of other people who care deeply
about it is invaluable.

The problem these days may be the opposite of the
one I encountered six years ago. It may be difficult to
choose which group to join, out of the many that are
working for change. What follows in this chapter are
some general guidelines to consider, drawn from my
own and others' experience. I will confess my own
bias: CCL has been *my* climate home for the last five

years. It is the group I go to most often for inspiration and support in my work. I believe in the CCL approach to ensuring a livable world. By empowering people to claim their personal and political power, CCL volunteers around the world are creating the political will needed to address the climate crisis. CCL work is transformational; it changes the volunteers lobbying as well as the politicians being lobbied. I'll share more on this later on in this chapter.

There are other groups doing phenomenal work. Most notable on the international scene are 350.org, the Climate Reality Leadership Corps, and the Transition Network.

We'll delve deeper into your potential climate match-ups later; first, let's talk about what to consider when looking for that perfect partnership.

Here are my top four "ingredients" to consider when searching for the right recipe for baking up some action on climate change. Because CCL is my favourite climate group, with just the right mix of ingredients for me, I refer to it throughout this discussion.

I offer these suggestions to help readers find the climate organization that suits their tastes the best. These tips can point the way, but like Liz Armstrong, each of you will be the best judge of when you've found the ingredients blended together in just the right way for your tastes.

Ingredients For Change

To avoid joining a half-baked organization, here's a list of four important elements to look for when checking out the climate groups to join:

HOPE

What is missing from much of the climate movement is hope. It has been a long and difficult fight against well-financed forces fiercely opposed to change. People who have been in the climate trenches for years may be battle-fatigued and cynical. While these emotions are honestly earned, right now the stakes are higher than ever before. The window to transformation is opening, and it is energy, enthusiasm, and creativity that are needed. Imagine the impact on the civil rights movement had Martin Luther King Jr given an "I Have a Nightmare" speech instead of his famous "I Have a Dream".

Look for an organization that welcomes new recruits warmly. It should offer inspiration and a clear vision of its goal along with a realistic assessment of our current situation. There should also be a healthy dose of fun in the mix, because it's hard to despair when you're having a good time.

"I feel hopeful for the first time in a long time," engineer and long-time climate activist Vivian Grove Fulks shared on Facebook after attending her first CCL conference and lobbying experience on Capitol Hill. It is possible to be involved in working for change on this issue *and* experience hope. It is, in fact, an essential part of the recipe for climate success.

INSPIRATION *AND* PERSPIRATION

Does the organization clearly articulate what it stands *for*, not just what it is against? You don't want your precious energy to go solely into opposing the status quo or specific projects; you want to be part of imagining and building a different and better future. Working for change often necessitates opposing something. North Americans concerned about global warming and preserving clean water have opposed the Keystone XL pipeline that would carry bitumen from the Alberta oil sands across the Ogallala Aquifer, the source of drinking water for over two million people and irrigation water for 30 percent of American agricultural land. But some of the groups against the pipeline went further than saying no to a risky fossil fuel project. They envisioned and took steps to create a renewable energy future that doesn't depend on dirty energy.

The proposed pipeline would cross the White Earth First Nation in Minnesota. The band has mounted strong resistance to the pipeline while at the same time taking steps to lessen their dependence on fossil fuels. Over the last several years three wind turbines and three solar projects have been installed on White Earth land. In a very forward-looking move, the band also partnered with Minnesota West Community College to train White Earth members to be Wind Energy Mechanics.

Bold Nebraska is a grassroots group mobilizing widespread opposition to Keystone XL pipeline among the state's ranchers and farmers. In 2013, Bold Nebraska crowd-funded the money needed to build, as they put it, "the clean energy future that we need." With the donated funds, the group built a wind turbine and solar-powered barn directly in the path of the proposed pipeline.

These are only a few of the examples of the groups not only resisting what we don't want but constructing a better future. These creative tactics can engage people in positive action, and are just what the climate movement needs.

> [Citizens Climate Lobby] is not just about climate change....It's about being able to come together and create a shared vision for building a better life.
>
> Amelia Potvin, Roaring Forks, Colorado CCL co-leader

STRUCTURE *AND* FLEXIBILITY

Does the group have a framework strong enough to support volunteers but flexible enough to allow scope for grassroots decision making and creativity? Individual volunteers appreciate different levels of support. Some people like to be given very specific tasks that can be repeated at regular intervals while other volunteers prefer being given the big picture goal along with the freedom to figure out how to get to it. The best organizations offer both options, as well as the companionship of like-minded individuals.

In CCL, there is only one hard and fast rule. When lobbying politicians, volunteers *must* show respect and gratitude for the elected official's public service. This rule applies to politicians of any political stripe, whether or not the climate lobbyist agrees with the elected official's priorities.

Beyond that one rule, there is a lot of scope for individual creativity. There's room for the outrageous in our climate work, CCL Executive Director Mark Reynolds has been known to tell volunteers, because it's not as crowded in that corner.

A Firm Foundation

As we move towards a fossil-fuel-free world that is also more democratic, inclusive, and respectful of differences, it's more important than ever that organizations working for change embody these principles. If the group uses divisive tactics and espouses an "us versus them" mentality, it is perpetuating the world view that got us into our difficulties in the first place. The "end justifies the means" way of doing business, including the business of social change, is no longer acceptable.

The movement led by Gandhi to expel the British from India and the American civil rights movement led by Martin Luther King Jr. are 20th century examples of being the change you want to see in the world. We in the climate movement can and must learn from these powerful and effective examples.

> As a satyagrahi [one who practises nonviolent resistance] never injures his opponent and always appeals, either to his reason...or his heart...satygraha is twice blessed; it blesses him who practises it, and him against whom it is practised.

Mahatma Gandhi

> Constructive ends can never give absolute moral justification to destructive means, because in the final analysis the end is preexistent in the mean.

Martin Luther King Jr.

At the launch of Citizens' Climate Lobby in 2007, founder Marshall Saunders summed up the CCL philosophy:

> *So the manner in which we will work with Congress is non-partisan, of course, but much, much more than that. It is respectful and generous in our appreciation of those who oppose us. It is patient and kind. This extends to how we think about people who disagree with us. And yet through all of the patience and kindness there is an indomitable will, never being defeated, never giving up.*

CCL's foundation is built on being the change we want to see in the world. It's this approach that offers the possibility of transforming both the volunteer lobbying for climate action and the politician being lobbied.

The Cowboy and Indian Alliance is another group modelling a new way of interacting with each other. In the spring of 2014, this unlikely coalition of tribal members, landowners, and ranchers rode by horseback to Washington D.C. United in their opposition to the Keystone XL pipeline, they camped out near the White House in a show of solidarity.

Climate Match: The Right Chemistry

It's time to introduce you to my climate "friends," those organizations that have kept me company on my journey as an advocate for a stable climate. These nine groups are at the forefront of leading change on global warming and creating a sustainable future. The first five groups are international in scope but encourage volunteers to engage locally. The final four are Canadian-based organizations, most of whom reach out beyond Canada's borders.

This is not meant to be an exhaustive list. It's an opportunity to peruse their profiles and choose which one, if any, is the right match for you. Don't forget to have some fun while you're sizing each other up!

International Climate Organizations

350.org

"The number 350 means climate safety: to preserve a livable planet, scientists tell us we must reduce the amount of CO_2 in the atmosphere from its current level of 400 parts per million to below 350 ppm. We believe that a global grassroots movement can hold our leaders accountable to the realities of science and the principles of justice. That movement is rising from the bottom up all over the world, and is uniting to create the solutions that will ensure a better future for all."

www.350.org

In 2009, 350.org was a large part of the inspiration that moved me from paralysis into action. On their website and in their videos, 350.org spelled out the climate crisis in a way that I could understand for the first time. They made it clear what needed to happen to preserve a safe climate for future generations: 350 ppm (parts per million) of carbon dioxide is the safe level of CO_2 in the atmosphere, and that's the level the world needs to return to.

Founded in 2009 by writer and environmentalist Bill McKibben and a handful of students from Middlebury College, 350.org's mandate is to build the first planet-wide, grassroots climate change movement. They have been extraordinarily successful. 350.org's first International Day of Climate Action in 2009 resulted in 5,200 simultaneous demonstrations in 181 countries, all calling for a return to 350 ppm level of CO_2. It was the most widespread day of political action in the world's history.

Six years later, 350.org has organized twenty thousand rallies in every country of the world except North Korea. They have also spearheaded the resistance to the now-stalled Keystone Pipeline that would transport bitumen from the Alberta oil sands through the heart of America to Texas. And on the heels of "Global Warming's Terrifying New Math", McKibben's viral 2012 article in Rolling Stone magazine, 350.org launched the fast-growing fossil fuel divestment movement (discussed separately in this chapter).

Find out more about their campaigns and get on 350.org's email list on their namesake website.

> *Telling the truth about climate change would require pulling away the biggest punchbowl in history, right when the party is in full swing. That's why the fight is so pitched. That's why those of us battling for the future need to raise our game. And it's why that view from the satellites, however beautiful from a distance, is likely to become ever harder to recognize as our home planet.*

Bill McKibben, *The Huffington Post*

CITIZENS' CLIMATE LOBBY

> *We're creating the political will for a livable world by empowering individuals to experience breakthroughs in exercising their personal and political power.*

www.citizensclimatelobby.org

CCL is a grassroots group with a twin focus: to create the political will for a livable planet and to empower people to claim their political and personal power. CCL's approach to changing the current political stalemate is based on a proven model developed by the poverty-reduction and citizen empowerment organization RESULTS. Unique in the climate arena, CCL's roots can also be traced to the principles of nonviolence and compassion that guided the social revolutions led by Mahatma Gandhi and Martin Luther King Jr.

Marshall Saunders is the gentle Texan giant who founded CCL in 2007. Saunders, a retired real estate broker, is an international philanthropist and winner of the 2009 Grameen Foundation Humanitarian Award. After retiring from business, he devoted two decades of his life to volunteer efforts focused on lifting the world's poorest people out of poverty with small micro-credit loans. In 2006, after watching *An Inconvenient Truth*, Saunders realized that global warming-related effects such as rising sea levels and more flooding and droughts were going to devastate many of the very people he had seen lift themselves out of poverty through micro-credit loans. After being trained by U.S. Vice President Gore's Climate Reality team, Saunders was compelled to do more.

I realized that anything my listeners intended to do as individuals was totally swamped by public policy, by what the government did or didn't do.

While I suggested ways for people to reduce their use of carbon, Congress extended a law that gave $18 billion in subsidies to oil and coal companies.

It seemed to me that Congress was doing things exactly backwards. Why? Because it is dominated by special interests, in this case the fossil fuel industry. In my heart I knew something else was at play: Ordinary people were not asking their members of Congress for anything regarding climate change, not in an organized and effective way. Furthermore, they didn't know what to do or how to do it, nor did they have the self-confidence and support they needed.

At the official launch of the first three chapters in San Diego, California in 2007, Saunders made CCL's Gandhian foundation clear. He emphasized the non-partisan nature of the organization. Lobbying elected officials was going to be done with a spirit of respect and cooperation, but also persistence.

Judging by the exponential growth of Saunders' organization, CCL is on to something special. Eighty CCL groups were added to the CCL global family in 2014 and in the first six months of 2015, 50 more came on board. By the summer of 2015, there were nearly 300 CCL chapters on four continents.

CCL volunteers concentrate on passing legislation that will put a price on carbon. The 9,000+ CCL members around the world lobby their elected representatives to pass a revenue-neutral carbon fee and dividend policy. This legislation would tax carbon polluters and return all of the revenues to households as dividends. Besides meeting with politicians, volunteers emphasize carbon fee and dividend in letters to the editor and opinion pieces in the media. CCL's laser focus is on creating the political will that's necessary for the U.S. Congress and other governments to support a revenue-neutral price on carbon.

Saunders, Executive Director Mark Reynolds, and the rest of the CCL team encourage every CCLer to embrace the work with care not only for the planet and each other, but also for those who oppose CCL's work.

I'm usually a fast learner, but it took me several years after joining CCL to absorb the group's unique approach to creating change. Before I could lobby the CCL way, I had to transform my "them and us" thinking to "us and us." I had to shift mental habits acquired over a lifetime. I needed to change *myself* before I could work for change on the climate issue the CCL way. This kind of climate work is deep personal work.

> *We're not for everybody. Some people would rather talk to other people about how unfair it is, how unjust, and how impossible it is and scream at the TV. We're not for those people. We're for the people who want to say "you know, this is my problem, I'm up to it, I'm willing to take it on. I understand it's hard but I'm up for the task."*

Mark Reynolds, Executive Director, Citizens' Climate Lobby

The Climate Reality Project

The Climate Reality Project is one of the world's leading organizations dedicated to mobilizing action around climate change. With a global movement more than 5 million strong and a grassroots network of trained Climate Reality Leaders, we are spreading the truth of the climate crisis to communities everywhere and creating cultural momentum to solve it.

www.24HoursofReality.org

Though the former Vice President has become a lightning rod for those on the political right to attack and deride, I believe Al Gore deserves nothing but praise for his tireless commitment to informing the public and policy makers about the climate crisis and the need to shift to an economy driven by clean energy. With the motto, "Get Smart, Get Loud, Get Active," the Climate Reality Project he founded focuses on training would-be climate educators and activists on the latest climate science and communication techniques. The goal is to have "world-changers" shaping the climate conversation at dinner tables and in communities around the world with a focus on solutions, not just science. Since 2010, the Climate Reality Project has also produced "24 Hours of Climate Reality," a live marathon broadcast featuring Gore, climate experts, and other prominent guests. The 2012 event, entitled "The Dirty Weather Report", drew 17 million online views and broke the world record for viewers of a live online event. It went on to win ten prestigious Telly Awards for excellence in online content.

To date, Climate Reality Corps has trained 8,000 people around the world to become climate leaders in their communities. Volunteers fill out an application to attend the three-day training event, and commit to making presentations in their community afterwards. There is no cost for the training itself, although volunteers are responsible for covering their own travel and accommodation costs.

I was lucky enough to be able to attend Climate Reality training in Toronto in the summer of 2015. It was both educational and inspirational. If you want to be familiar with, and continually updated on, the latest climate science and solutions, this training is one of the best ways to do it.

To find out more about the Climate Reality Project, and learn when the next training is offered, visit www.climaterealityproject.org.

> Today, climate change is standing in the way of a healthy tomorrow for all of us. But at Climate Reality, we know that practical solutions are right in front of us. We can create a healthy, sustainable, and prosperous future by making a planet-wide shift from dirty fossil fuels to clean, reliable, and affordable renewable energy.
>
> www.24HoursofReality.org

Fossil Fuel Divestment Movement

It doesn't make sense to invest my retirement money in a company whose business plan means there won't be an Earth to retire on.

Bill McKibben, "Do The Math"

In November 2012, 350.org launched a massively successful cross-America "Do The Math" tour. "Do The Math" refers to the climate math that tells us that globally, we can emit 565 more gigatons of carbon dioxide and still stay below 2 degrees Celcius of warming. If we emit more than that, we will be in the realm of catastrophic climate change. The problem is that oil, gas, and coal industries currently have enough fossil fuel in their reserves to emit five times that amount: 2,795 gigatons of carbon dioxide. And their economic bottom line requires them to burn it all.

That math is why 350.org started a divestment campaign to make investing money in fossil fuels as undesirable to governments, schools, and faith institutions as investing in South Africa became during the anti-apartheid movement in the 1980s. Divestment simply means withdrawing money from stocks, bonds, or other funds that are unethical or immoral. The movement for fossil fuel divestment (sometimes called disinvestment), is asking institutions to move their money out of oil, coal, and gas companies for both moral and financial reasons. Both the United Nations and prominent individuals such as Archbishop Desmond Tutu have put their support behind the fast-growing divestment movement. The president of the World Bank, Jim Yong Kim, has stated that "every company, investor and bank that screens new and existing investments for climate risk is simply being pragmatic."

The successful South African divestment movement eroded the credibility of the apartheid regime in that country and is lauded for its part in the system's ultimate dismantling. After a start in the late 1970s on a handful of university campuses, by the mid-1980s 155 university and college campuses had divested from companies doing business in South Africa. The movement went on to influence 22 countries, 26 state governments, and 90 cities to withdraw their money from companies associated with the apartheid regime.

> *Fossil fuel divestment takes the fossil fuel industry to task for its culpability in the climate crisis. By naming this industry's singularly destructive influence - and by highlighting the moral dimensions of climate change- we hope that the fossil fuel divestment movement can help break the hold that the fossil fuel industry has on our economy and our governments.*

www.gofossilfree.org

While 350.org launched the divestment movement, there is now an international, grassroots network of campaigns working on divestment projects. Many of these are independently run and their focus may vary slightly depending on the local contexts. Most of them, though, are asking institutions to:

- Immediately freeze any new investment in fossil fuel companies.

- Divest from direct ownership and any commingled funds that include fossil fuel public equities and corporate bonds within five years.

Recent high profile organizations to divest from fossil fuels include dozens of religious institutions, including the World Council of Churches and the Lutheran World Federation. Stanford University's Board of Trustees recently announced that they are divesting from 100 coal companies. In 2014 the University of Glasgow's board voted unanimously to begin divesting its entire endowment, worth over $200 million U.S. dollars. Several high-profile charitable foundations, including one belonging to the heirs to the Rockefeller oil fortune, have started to divest. Cities such as San Francisco, Seattle, and Oslo have also committed to withdraw their investments from fossil fuels.

Find out more about getting involved in or starting a divestment movement in your community at www.go-fossilfree.org.

We can't bankrupt Exxon. But we can politically and morally bankrupt them.

Bill McKibben, "Do The Math"

TRANSITION NETWORK

A push towards clean air, sunshine, beauty, rediscovering each other; community and celebration. This is a key shift in our perception. The difference between change that feels like being torn away from something and change that feels like moving towards something is huge. This is the approach Transition takes. It suggests that collective intentional transition could lead us to a far better place than where we are today. Who's to say that the world we see today is the best we could ever do?

Rob Hopkins, Founder, Transition Network

From two small and very local initiatives in Kinsale, Ireland and Totnes, UK, the Transition Town idea has spread across the globe in just eight years. As of April 2014, there were more than 1,120 registered Transition initiatives in 43 countries representing thousands of people working together to create awareness of climate change and peak oil and set up a huge range of locally-inspired and creative projects.

Our family has been involved in Transition Red Lake (TRL) since its unofficial launch in 2011. TRL serves as an umbrella group to support people and groups working towards increasing our community's resiliency. The initiatives that have developed under TRL's umbrella include three community gardens, a clothes swap, a "permablitz" gardening installation, a cheese-making workshop, seed swaps, and organized garden tours. Every Wednesday, volunteers organize a community kitchen where people gather to share local organic food and to swap stories and recipes.

> *Transition Red Lake is a group of local people working towards increasing our community's capacity to look after ourselves, our land, and our water.*

> www.transitionredlake.wordpress.com

Transition Towns, which has grown into the Transition Network, sprang out of the work of Rob Hopkins, a permaculture and natural building educator from Britain. Hopkins was teaching at Kinsale College in 2003 when he first learned about peak oil. Peak oil is the recognition that since oil is a non-renewable resource, there will be a point in the future (or the recent past, some argue) at which the rate of global oil extraction will hit a peak and then decline. Experts no longer debate *if* this will occur, only *when*. What isn't debated is the huge economic as well as sociopolitical impact this decline will have on a world economy powered by oil.

Hopkins and his students set to work designing an "Energy Descent Plan" for their community to wean itself off of fossil fuels which was later adopted by Kinsale as official municipal policy. After moving back to Britain, it was in 2006 that Hopkins started Transition Town Totnes as a localized response to the challenges of peak oil and climate change. Transition Totnes and the thousands of other Transition initiatives that it has inspired around the world are focused on increasing the resilience of their communities. Resilience is defined by the Transition movement as the ability of a system (whether an individual, family, community, or an entire economy) to hold together and maintain its ability to function when faced with sudden change and shocks from the outside. The Transition movement encourages all of us to view the coming shift away from oil dependency and high-carbon living not as a movement *away* from something, but rather a push *towards* something:

> *Rebuilding local agriculture and food production, localising energy production, rethinking health-care, rediscovering local building materials in the context of zero energy building, rethinking how we manage waste, all build resilience and offer the potential of an extraordinary renaissance - economic, cultural, and spiritual. I am not afraid of a world with less consumerism, less 'stuff', and no economic growth. Indeed, I am far more frightened of the opposite.*

Rob Hopkins, *The Transition Handbook*

The Transition movement is an invitation to each of us to move out of fear of the future and join other people and communities around the globe who are taking the future into their own hands. Right here and now they are taking concrete steps towards creating a more abundant and nourishing tomorrow.

Hopkins has authored several excellent books on transition, including *The Transition Handbook: From oil dependency to local resilience* and *The Transition Companion: Making your community more resilient in uncertain times*. To learn more about Transition Network, and to find out if there is a Transition initiative close to you, explore their website at www.transitionnetwork.org.

CANADIAN CLIMATE CAMPAIGNS

BLUE DOT CAMPAIGN

> *The Blue Dot movement is a growing national grassroots initiative based on the idea that everyone in Canada deserves the right to enjoy fresh air, clean water and safe food. As Canadians, we don't have these rights. We want to show our elected representatives that our town is ready to be a leader on environmental rights and to begin changing our laws so they protect the people and places we love. Do you think it's something you can support?*
>
> www.bluedot.ca

In the fall of 2014 scientist, broadcaster, and internationally renowned environmentalist David Suzuki toured across Canada to inspire a movement to enshrine environmental rights in the Canadian constitution. The Blue Dot campaign is aimed at generating widespread support for the right to a healthy environment at the municipal level. The hope is that it will have a domino effect on higher levels of government that will culminate in recognition in the Canadian Charter of Rights and Freedoms. Impressively, in less than a year since its launch, nearly 80,000 Canadians have joined Suzuki's campaign. These volunteers have mobilized 73 municipal governments to pass declarations recognizing the right of their citizens to fresh air, clean water, and healthy food.

The David Suzuki Foundation is coordinating the Blue Dot campaign and providing practical support for volunteers who sign up to organize in their local community. To find out more or to get involved, visit www.bluedot.ca.

> *Across the country, Canadians believe in our inherent right to a healthy environment – clean water, fresh air, healthy food and a say in decisions that affect us. One by one, people like you stand up to say this right should be recognized.*
>
> www.bluedot.ca

CLIMATE FAST

What did you do once you knew?

Drew Dillinger, *The Hieroglyphic Stairway*

ClimateFast is a focused group of concerned and dedicated volunteers whose motto is "Hungry For Change." Started in 2012 with a 12-day fast, they strive to persuade Canadian parliamentarians to take urgent and substantial action on climate change. The group goes to Parliament Hill in Ottawa annually, to lobby MPs and Senators to sign the ClimateFast Pledge for Politicians. This pledge asks elected officials to commit to ending fossil fuel subsidies, putting a price on carbon, and supporting the development of a renewable energy plan for Canada.

ClimateFast invites people to join them on a food or carbon fast on the first day of each month. Go to www.climatefast.ca to learn more about their campaign. You can sign up for their newsletter and also access their resources for submitting letters to the editor and for contacting politicians.

If you are outside of Canada and would like to get involved in this movement, visit the www.FastForTheClimate.org website. Similar to the Canadian-based ClimateFast, FastForTheClimate is an international group that sprang up in response to Philippine Climate Commissioner Yeb Sano's emotional plea at the UN Climate Talks in Warsaw in 2013. In response to the devastation of his country by Super Typhoon Haiyan during those talks, Sano said he would fast until the Warsaw conference ended or delivered actions that would "stop the madness" of the climate crisis.

> In solidarity with my countrymen who are struggling to find food back home and with my brother who has not had food for the last three days, in all due respect Mr. President, and I mean no disrespect for your kind hospitality, I will now commence a voluntary fasting for the climate. This means I will voluntarily refrain from eating food during this COP until a meaningful outcome is in sight.

Philippine Climate Commissioner Yeb Sano, COP19

OUR HORIZON

> If there is any product that merits a warning label, this is it. Climate change is the greatest challenge of our time; if we don't even have the courage to put a simple sticker on a gas pump, what hope do we have in actually addressing the problem?

Rob Shirkey, Executive Director, Our Horizon

Launched in 2013 by Toronto-based lawyer Rob Shirkey, the national non-profit organization Our Horizon's innovative approach to climate action is to focus on lobbying municipal governments to require warning labels about climate and air pollution on all gas pumps. Not a new idea, the labels would be similar to tobacco labels which are now found around the world; labels which have been shown to change consumer behavior and attitudes.

Our Horizon is garnering strong support from academics and NGOs such as the David Suzuki Foundation and the Canadian Association of Physicians for the Environment. The B.C. municipalities of West and North Vancouver along with the regional body representing 51 municipalities on Vancouver Island have voted to endorse the labelling of gas pumps in their regions.

If you are intrigued by Shirkey's idea and want to learn more, go to www.ourhorizon.org or email supporters@ourhorizon.org.

> *Our vision is to continue to create precedents in North American communities and take these examples of leadership to the United Nations' COP21 climate change conference in Paris this December to share with delegates from around the globe. With similar labels on tobacco packages all over the world, this idea has been primed to go global. The idea is perhaps the lowest cost climate intervention in the world yet has the potential to be among the most impactful.*

> www.OurHorizon.org

Time for Change Action Step

Join other climate-concerned citizens. Don't wait.

Establish a timeline for choosing your climate partner. Here are the steps you can take to make a match happen:

1. Set yourself a firm deadline for joining a group in your area or online. Get out your favourite calendar, electronic or paper. Choose the date you are setting as your goal, and circle it on your calendar. Put in reminders every week leading up to that date.

2. Write down the four traits to look for in a climate group: hope, having a positive vision, both structure and flexibility for volunteers, and embodying the change we want to see. Are there any characteristics you would add or eliminate from this list?

3. Establish the amount of time you have available. Write this down underneath the date you set as your goal in step one. Keep both commitments in a place you can refer to regularly. Do you have two hours a month? Half an hour a week? Be specific; for example "45 minutes on Monday morning before getting the kids up for school." Being under-committed won't help your health or the planet, but neither will over-commitment. Your time available may go up or down depending on your circumstances. It's not set it stone, but it's best to have a firm idea at the onset.

If attending regular meetings is difficult because of your schedule, consider what skills you have that you could contribute to the organization on your own time. Are you artistic, good at networking or with a computer? Maybe fundraising is one of your talents? Or perhaps you can join a sub-committee that meets at a different time that works better for you. Don't give up on becoming part of something bigger because at first glance your schedules don't mesh.

4. Next, do some information-gathering. Explore the websites of the organizations you are interested in; if they have an office in your community, you may want to stop in. Once you have found one or more that meet the criteria you established in steps one to three, take the relationship to the next level. Speak to someone in the organization, either on the phone or in person. Have questions prepared that will help you decide if this organization has the potential to be the right climate match for you.

5. Once you've completed the first four actions, it's time to attend a meeting or event. Find out the date and time of the next group gathering and plan to attend. Add it to your calendar, along with reminders the day before and day of the event.

6. After you've attended a meeting, reflect back on the traits of a good climate organization listed in step one. Does this group meet your criteria? If

not, go back to step two and repeat until you have found a good match.

Setting deadlines is important to maintain momentum. It is what turns good intentions into action. Make that timeline and fill in the steps. Keep your goals visible until your head, heart, and feet are engaged in creating a healthy future for the planet *and* yourself!

How much time will climate group therapy take? That will differ from group to group. It's up to you to have a clear idea of the time you have available, and stick to it once you find an organization that suits you. Before you join, they should be able to give you an approximation of the time commitment required. For example, being a Citizens' Climate Lobby volunteer requires a minimum of four hours a month. This tally reflects the time required to attend the monthly meeting, and write two letters to the editor or attend one meeting with an elected official.

This book promises that you can fit these climate action steps into the time it takes to attend a weekly yoga class or watch two of your favorite TV shows. This includes connecting with other climate-concerned folks. Don't opt out of joining a group because you are concerned about the time commitment. Studies show that people who volunteer their time have an increased sense of life satisfaction and well being along with a reduced rate of depression. Not only that, some research suggests that those who give of their time for selfless reasons, such as helping others (or saving the planet), live longer than those who don't volunteer. It's possible you may recoup every minute of the time you spend volunteering!

Although it doesn't provide the same health benefits as volunteering your time does, it may be that your support comes not through joining activities but in supporting a climate group financially or other ways. A volunteer for a community group I belonged to approved of our goals but, with a young family, didn't have the time to come out to our monthly meetings. Instead she volunteered to be our treasurer. In this way she offered the group a valuable service without needing to attend meetings. Do you have a skill you can offer to a group that you can work into your schedule?

If the groups mentioned in this chapter don't provide you with your own "bingo!" moment, go online and fire up your search engine. No matter what climate group you join, make sure your head, heart, and feet are engaged. Creating a livable future doesn't require joyless activism. There's truth in the cliché that yesterday is gone, tomorrow is in the future, but today is a gift; that's why it's called the present. Even though this work is focused on creating a better future, it should be life-giving in the here and now. It should be work that lights you *and* the world up.

When asked if I am pessimistic or optimistic about the future, my answer is always the same: If you look at the science about what is happening on Earth and aren't pessimistic, you don't understand data. But if you meet the people who are working to restore this Earth and the lives of the poor, and you aren't optimistic, you haven't got a pulse. What I see everywhere in the world are ordinary people willing to confront despair, power, and incalculable odds in order to restore some semblance of grace, justice, and beauty to this world.

Paul Hawkens, University of Portland
Commencement Address

Good News for a Change

China's Great Green Wall

China is not only the world's most populated country, it has the dubious distinction of being the world's largest emitter of greenhouse gases. What is less well known is what China is doing to tackle climate change and its air pollution problem. The country is serious about building the world's largest clean energy system. In 2014 China was the largest investor in renewable energy in the world ($89.5 billion, or 29% of all global renewable energy investment).

In northern China, a "great green wall" of trees is being planted. This massive tree planting project has helped to offset global forest decline and has sucked some climate-changing carbon dioxide out of the atmosphere. Experts found that between 2003 and 2012, China's reforestation efforts, along with regrowth on abandoned farmland in Russia, have helped offset most of the carbon storage lost from tropical deforestation. In that decade, carbon storage in Chinese forests increased by almost one billion tons.

CHAPTER 4

Nature Therapy:
Spending Time with Mother Nature

Hope is the thing with feathers

Emily Dickenson

Think back to your own childhood. Did you have opportunities to run around your neighbourhood, ride your bike, and play unsupervised in parks and backyards? Did you attend summer camps where campers were allowed unstructured time to play outdoors? Many of us did. But times have changed. These days, in our increasingly urbanized society, most of us are suffering from a lack of time in nature. Children in particular are at risk. With electronic distractions, academic pressures, and a full slate of extracurricular activities, outdoor play time for kids is often left out. Yet without any time in nature, we lose touch with the natural world. We forget we are animals; sophisticated and intelligent mammals, but still a part of the animal world. It's only very recently, in the history of the human species, that we have become insulated from nature's rhythms.

Fourteen years ago our family moved from a prairie city of 750,000 to a community of 5,000 in the woods of northern Ontario. We live on a lake surrounded by boreal forest. There are lots of rocks, trees, and water but no shopping malls or movie theaters. Fox, deer, and bear occasionally stroll through our yard.

A few years after we moved to Red Lake, my husband Mark decided to get our family even further out in the wilderness in a canoe. I resisted initially; okay, I was downright cranky about it! I made the sensible argument that we lived on a lake. We had comfortable beds for sleeping and a well-appointed kitchen for cooking. Putting in the enormous time and effort required to transport the four of us, all our sleeping gear, and food just to spend time sleeping in a tent by a different lake a few hours away seemed silly. Mark persisted, enticing me by buying the most comfortable camping mattress available and letting me bring along my kayak.

A decade later, I'm grateful for Mark's perseverance. Our now-adult children have vivid memories of our canoe-ing adventures, and most of them are good! Canoe trips with friends have given us many belly laughs along with moments of exasperation. We've shivered under our boats waiting for storms to pass; we've watched north-ern lights dance over a still lake. Loons have sung us to sleep and yes, mosquitoes have delighted in our delicate skin. Our family has established life-long connections to each other and to the natural world.

My time in the wild renews my spirit. I come back re-freshed and able to once again step into the fray of life. The nourishment of deep drinks from the well of nature's beauty feeds my commitment to do my part to ensure there is a livable world for future generations.

A Deficit of Wildness

In his 2005 book *Last Child in the Woods*, Robert Louv coined the term "nature deficit disorder" to describe the loss of connection with the outdoors that children experience these days. Louv's latest book, *The Nature Principle*, acknowledges that adults are also susceptible to this disconnection. For most of our species' history, humans spent their lives outside, not cooped up inside four walls. Our ancestors were adept at predicting the weather by reading nature's signs. They planted crops by the waxing and waning of the moon. Previous generations' lives moved to the cadence of the natural world, putting them in touch with its intricate rhythms. Yet the majority of humans these days live urban lives detached from the natural world.

The increasing incidence of nature deficit disorder is happening at the same time that researchers are finding evidence of the health benefits of time spent in nature. People who spend time outdoors tend to be more creative, have better functioning immune systems, and lower blood pressure compared to their more housebound counterparts. Along with the stress-busting benefit of more physical activity, time in nature lowers heart rates and promotes a relaxation response. Both adults and kids are less stressed after spending time outside. Children who play outdoors regularly have better distance vision than those who primarily play indoors. Studies suggest that children with ADHD seem to focus better after being outside. Although the reasons may not be completely clear yet, research (and intuition) suggests that natural green spaces are calming and soothing to the soul.

There are more than just health benefits to time in nature. A love of nature learned early results in adults who are good stewards of the planet. In her book *Partnering with Nature,* Catriona MacGregor argues that we will "be able to solve problems, such as global warming, when we gain greater awareness about who and what we are in relation to the Earth and other living creatures."

Our disconnection from nature has made it difficult to comprehend the reality of global warming even as signs of its impact increase. Indigenous people who remain more connected to the natural world know there is a problem. At the 2010 World Religions Summit, Katherine Whitecloud, an aboriginal leader from the Dakota First Nation in Manitoba and a descendant of Chief Sitting Bull, spoke these powerful words to the gathered religious leaders, "We are foolishly and arrogantly raping Mother Earth so She has nothing left to offer...Mother Earth is crying, attempting to rid herself of all the toxins we have poured into her." She reminded the room that the rivers are the veins of Mother Earth, and those veins are being poisoned. Whitecloud's words echo the warning of Lakota Chief Luther Standing Bear who said a century earlier that "man's heart, away from nature, becomes hard; [the Lakota] knew lack of respect for growing, living things soon led to lack of respect for humans too."

Family Therapy with Mother Nature

The Earth is called Mother Nature for a reason. Like all good mothers, she takes care of us; time outside nurtures both our bodies and spirits. We are orphans not by her choice but by ours. It's time for us to allow nature to wrap her arms around us, to slow down our racing minds and pulses. As I found on our summer canoe trips, it's never too late to reconnect with nature. Although Mark knew nothing about "nature deficit disorder" when he began his mission to get our family out of doors and into a canoe, his instinct was right on. While a wilderness canoe trip may not be for everyone, walks in a city park or a day at the beach are also therapy for nature deficit disorder.

The challenge is to prioritize unstructured time outside in our busy schedules. The good news is that much of this therapy is low-cost or free. And it can be a lot of fun. It may be easier to make room on our iPhone calendars if we remember Robert Lour's assertion that time in nature is *not* leisure time. It is a vital investment in our children's health and also our own. I would add that it's also an essential investment in a stable climate for future generations.

> *Are you feeling tired, irritable, stressed out? Well you might consider NatureRx. From the people that brought you "Getting Outside" comes prescription-strength NatureRx, a non-harmful medication shown to relieve the crippling systems of modern life. Nature's recommended for humans of all ages, and it's great for pets, too...Side effects may include spontaneous euphoria, taking yourself less seriously, and being in a good mood for no apparent reason.*
>
> www.nature-rx.org

Our Bodies, Our Planet

In his best-selling book *The Body Keeps The Score*, Harvard psychiatrist and trauma specialist Dr. Bessel van der Kolk discusses how traumatized people often disassociate from their bodies. A massage therapist described to me how a paramedic stressed by difficult scenes he had witnessed at work was initially unable to feel her hands massaging his limbs. Dr. van der Kolk's work confirms that this disconnection from the body happens when what we have been through is too painful to feel.

At this point in history the majority of us have collectively disassociated from the body that sustains life, the Earth. Our individual bodies can't survive without the water, air, and food that the Earth provides us. Yet as a society we are filling the rivers, oceans, land, and atmosphere with toxins. This suicidal behavior is painful to bear witness to. I believe that most of us are traumatized by what is happening to our environment, whether or not we realize it. Buddhist scholar and eco-philosopher Joanna Macy's work, which she calls "The Work that Reconnects", recognizes that trauma. In workshops and through her books, Macy has inspired thousands of people to move through the pain they feel about what is happening to the Earth and to take heart. After acknowledging the pain, they are often inspired to work together to create a livable future.

Part of the "unfreezing" work that we can do is re-connecting to the body of the Earth through our own bodies. Simple practices that make us more conscious of our bodies can be very helpful. Meditation and walking are two of the easiest and most accessible ways to improve our body awareness. Dr. van der Kolk's research has shown that doing yoga and participating in improvisational theatre are effective in reducing the symptoms of posttraumatic stress disorder (PTSD). They can reconnect us to our bodies.

Consider ways that you can consciously appreciate your body more. It may not be perfect, but every day the trillions of cells contained within it are involved in a marvelous dance of homeostasis to sustain your life. We truly are "fearfully and wonderfully made", as Psalm 139 says. Yet it seems easier to focus on what we don't like about our physique and put off appreciating it until we've lost ten pounds or run that marathon. Valuing our bodies as they are now doesn't mean we can't lose weight or exercise, but rather it changes the focus of the experience. Instead of punishing ourselves into exercising or dieting, getting into better shape can become a way of loving ourselves. When we accept our bodies as they are, it becomes easier to make healthy food and exercise choices. A strong and positive relationship to our own body makes connecting to our larger body, the Earth, much easier.

When you arise in the morning, think of what a privilege it is to be alive: to breathe, to think, to feel, to love.

Marcus Aurelius

Time for Change Action Step

Begin immediately to plan regular time outside. In fact, start now by putting put down this book, lacing up your shoes, and going for a walk in the greenest part of your neighborhood.

Schedule time outside every day; have fun by yourself, with your dog, or with friends or family. Make sure there is play involved. Your family will take their cue from you; if you are relaxed and enjoying yourself, they will, too. On the other hand, if they pick up that you are outside because it's an obligation rather than a pleasure, things will go downhill quickly. If it feels like a family hike up a mountain is too much work, find something easier and more appealing. Maybe you can commit to a walk around the neighbourhood for 15 minutes after supper. Plan a picnic lunch on your lawn on Saturdays. Play catch outside. Blow bubbles. Plan a scavenger hunt. Get creative!

Part of getting in touch with nature is scheduling regular computer and television sabbaticals into your family's week. Family members may complain initially, but they will thank you down the road for the memories created through technology breaks

Our family loves to incorporate food into our outdoor experiences; we've spent many hours at u-pick strawberry farms and picking wild blueberries in the bush. Wiener roasts and picnics are also a good reason to gather outside. Gardening, a fantastic way for kids and adults to connect with nature and her rhythms, is becoming increasingly popular and accessible. Even apartment dwellers have the opportunity to get their hands in the dirt, thanks to the proliferation of community gardens that rent plots and grow social connections at the same time.

If your kids attend summer camp, look for one that includes some unstructured time outside. Or perhaps putting up a tent in your backyard is more your family's style. Lying outside and star gazing is a free and awe-inspiring experience.

Make a conscious decision to be kind to your own body, starting with expressing gratitude to your cells for keeping you alive. Thanks to their unsung work, you are able to be here now.

Getting outside requires a time commitment. But spending time in nature is more than just fresh air and blue sky; it's an investment in improving your health and (if you get outside with family and friends) your relationships. If you already spend regular time appreciating the outdoors, give yourself a pat on the back (hopefully while you're outside appreciating the sun on your shoulders or the stars above your head). The benefits of spending time outside are exponential. To the health benefits of a walk in the park you can add building memories along with creating a better world for future generations. That's pretty good payback, however you look at it. Mother Nature approves.

Good News for a Change

Michelle Obama has done a lot to boost the popularity of gardening after installing a White House Kitchen Garden in her first year as First Lady. Gardening is an integral part of Mrs. Obama's "Let's Move" initiative to raise a healthier generation of American children. Whether it's due to the Obama Effect or not, the number of home gardens in America is increased dramatically. In 2013 there were 33 million more home gardens in the U.S. than in 2008, a 200% increase. In that same time the number of community gardens in the nation tripled, from one million to three million. Before attending the annual planting of the White House Kitchen Garden in 2014, Mike Metallo, president and CEO of the National Gardening Association stated "...there truly is a food revolution taking place in America."

"At a time of economic crisis, a garden can provide a surprisingly large amount of fresh, healthy produce," Author and food activist Michael Pollan told ABC News after the Obamas announced their plan for a vegetable garden. "But just as important, it teaches important habits of mind -- helping people to reconnect with their food, eat more healthily on a budget and recognize that we're less dependent on the industrial food chain, and cheap fossil fuel, than we assume."

CHAPTER 5

Science Matters:
Know the Consensus

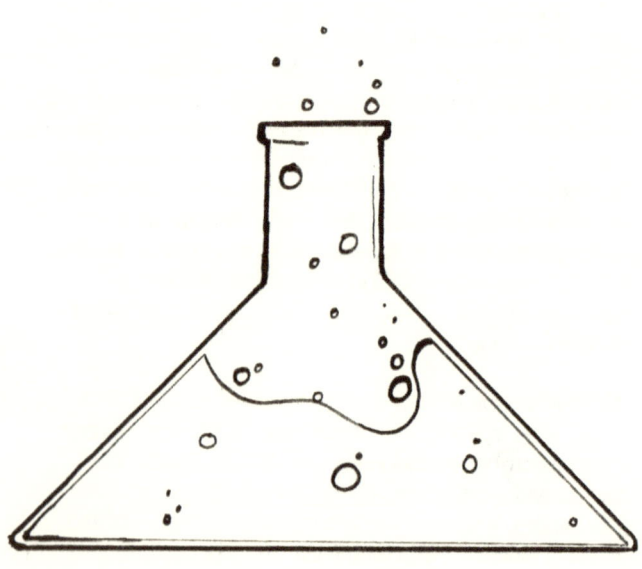

To be an effective agent for change on global warming, a person doesn't need to be a climate scientist. We can ground our concern in the understanding that **97 percent of climate scientists agree, based on the evidence, that global warming is happening and it is human-caused**. Knowing this qualifies every one of us who is concerned about preserving a livable world for future generations to speak up on their behalf.

Starting with that foundation, what else could be added to a climate-concerned citizen's toolkit?

There's an almost inexhaustible amount of books and websites out there offering excellent information on climate change and renewable energy. Before evaluating a few of those resources, let's add an important list to your toolbox. There are a growing number of prominent businesses, scientific associations, and other organizations issuing statements concurring with the scientific consensus on global warming. Many of these are also calling for governments to place an effective price on carbon pollution as an important step towards addressing global warming.

- U.S. Department of Defense
- U.S. Navy
- National Oceanic and Atmospheric Administration (NOAA)
- National Aeronautics and Space Agency (NASA)
- Royal Meteorological Society (UK)

- World Meteorological Society
- Agricultural organizations such as the Crop Science Society of America and the Soil Science Society of America
- Munich Re & Swiss Re, the world's largest re-insurance companies
- American Medical Association
- Ducks Unlimited and the Sportsman's Advisory Group on Climate Change
- Pope Francis and the Pontifical Academy of Science
- International Monetary Fund (IMF)
- International Energy Agency (IEA)
- World Bank
- Canada's EcoFiscal Commission
- National Roundtable on the Environment and the Economy (Canada)
- International Aid agencies such as World Vision, Oxfam, and the Mennonite Central Committee.

These organizations, and a growing number of others, are raising the alarm about global warming. There is agreement about the severity and urgency of the threat. Scientific associations, along with an increasing number of businesses and international agencies, are calling for swift action to decrease the world's carbon emissions to preserve a stable climate for future generations. Climate-concerned citizens are in good company when we call on our governments to act on climate change.

Websites Are Not Created Equal: Navigating the Internet

Sources of accurate information are required in every climate toolbox. What non-experts like me, and possibly you, need to know is where to turn to get factual data and analysis of trends when we want them. Physicians turn to internet databases when an unusual medical problem presents itself, so there's no reason that climate-concerned folks can't do the same. A word of caution though; one needs to be *very* wary of blogs that claim to be a source of climate information but are not sourced from reliable science-based websites or journals. Common sense isn't as common as one would think. In these days of free-for-all information exchange on the internet, not all websites are created equal. You wouldn't be reassured if you found out your physician was turning to Joe the Plumber's blog for advice on your rash. The same standard should be applied to the complex global climate system. Any website or blog that disagrees with the consensus of every National Academy of Science on the planet, with all but one of the 9,136 authors of peer-reviewed science papers published between November 2012 to December 2013, with the Canadian Meteorological Society, with NASA, etc., must have solid links to well-researched data to back up its outlier claims (spoiler alert: such a website doesn't exist).

Choosing a Climate School

You've got the firm foundation of the scientific consensus underneath you. If you choose to become more informed about global warming, here are some suggestions for reputable climate "schools" in which to enroll. You will recognize some crossover from the Climate Match discussion in Chapter Three. CCL and Climate Reality not only offer a possible climate home, they also offer excellent climate education resources. It's fine to mix and match until you get just the right combination for you.

CITIZENS' CLIMATE LOBBY MONTHLY CALLS

Citizens' Climate Lobby (CCL) holds an international teleconference call once a month which focuses on education, celebration of volunteer accomplishments, and practical inspiration to action. The meeting, on the first Saturday at 1:00 pm EST, hosts a distinguished guest with expertise in global warming. Past speakers include Rear Admiral Len Hering (ret.) of the United States Navy; Scott Nystrom, Senior Economic Associate at Regional Economic Modeling Inc (REMI); author and director of the climate science unit at Texas Tech University Dr. Katharine Hayhoe; Anthony Leiserowitz from the Yale Project on Climate Change Communication; renowned climate scientist and author Dr James Hansen, and Eli Lehrer, President of R Street Institute.

Past CCL calls are available on their website, www. citizensclimatelobby.org or on iTunes. If you are interested in listening to the calls live and connecting with a CCL group close to you, email ccl@citizensclimatelobby.org. Along with the climate education you'll get by joining the CCL live calls, the encouragement and connection with other people who are passionate about creating a livable world is invaluable.

CLIMATE REALITY TRAINING

Al Gore's Climate Reality Leadership Corps training provides volunteers with top-notch education and resources in climate science, communications, and organizing. The three-day trainings are held several times a year in the United States and other locations around the world. There is no cost to attend the training once you've been accepted, but individuals are responsible to cover the cost of their travel and accommodation.

As of 2015, 8,000 people around the world have been trained to be Climate Reality Leaders. If you have a chance to attend one of these, take it. In 2015 training was offered in Toronto, only the second time Climate Reality has come to Canada. I was lucky enough to attend. The quality of the speakers, including Vice President Gore, was outstanding and the follow-up resources provided to trainees are superb. Part of becoming a Climate Reality Leader is committing to perform 10 "acts of leadership" within a year. These outreach activities can be as varied as giving a presentation, writing a letter to the editor, organizing a film screening, or meeting with an elected official.

GLOBAL CLIMATE CHANGE: VITAL SIGNS OF THE PLANET

In an exciting announcement in the fall of 2015, NASA confirmed that they had found evidence of water on Mars. Not only are they the best resource on the planet for space information and exploration, NASA scientists have a wealth of knowledge on the Earth's climate system. If you want robust scientific data, www.climate. nasa.gov is a great go-to website. Among the "vital signs" displayed prominently on their home page are current carbon dioxide levels, global temperature increase since 1880, decrease in summer arctic ice, land ice loss on Antarctica and Greenland, sea level rise over the last 100 years, and loss of global forest cover since 2000 as identified from satellite data. Clicking on each vital sign will take you to more in-depth scientific data.

Also easily accessed on NASA's climate website is a quick summary of global warming facts, broken down into categories of evidence, causes, effects, scientific consensus, and frequently asked questions. Their "climate kids" section, available under the drop-down resources link, breaks down into different aspects of the world's climate system into various topics linked to kid-friendly games, information, and crafts.

NASA is a world leader in climate studies and Earth science. While its role is not to set climate policy or prescribe particular responses or solutions to climate change, its purview does include providing the robust scientific data needed to understand climate change. NASA then makes this information available to the global community – the public, policy- and decision-makers and scientific and planning agencies around the world.

www.climate.nasa.gov

GETTING SKEPTICAL ABOUT GLOBAL WARMING SKEPTICISM

Another helpful website is skepticalscience.com. It focuses on explaining climate change science and rebutting misinformation. Real scientific questioning is a good thing, their website reminds us, but that's not what those who oppose climate action are up to.

Scientific skepticism is healthy. Scientists should always challenge themselves to improve their understanding. Yet this isn't what happens with climate change denial. Skeptics vigorously criticise any evidence that supports man-made global warming and yet embrace any argument, op-ed, blog or study that purports to refute global warming. This website gets skeptical about global warming skepticism. Do their arguments have any scientific basis? What does the peer reviewed scientific literature say?

www.skepticalscience.com

One helpful aspect of Skeptical Science is its straightforward explanations. With a click of the mouse, a reader can choose the category of responses to 176 common climate myths. Answers start with basic science and escalate in complexity to intermediate and advanced.

Skeptical Science also has a temperature trend calculator which some people will find interesting and helpful. Its purpose is to aid readers in evaluating unsubstantiated claims by some climate deniers about temperature trends (i.e. "the Earth is cooling").

Skeptical Science is a blog, and was created not by a climate scientist but a climate communicator, John Cook. It is, however, linked to both the International Panel on Climate Change (IPCC) and NASA, and each new blog posting includes multiple links to peer-reviewed scientific journals. It passes the "well-sourced" test for a reputable climate blog.

> The good thing about science is that it's true whether you believe it or not.

> Neil DeGrasse Tyson, Astrophysicist

Caring For Creation: Faith-based Resources

"Climate change represents one of the principal challenges facing humanity in our day," states *Laudato Si: On Care For Our Common Home*.

As I write this it's been only a few months since the release of Pope Francis's encyclical on creation care and already its clarion call to action is creating a stir inside and outside the Catholic Church. Two months later, an Islamic declaration on climate change was issued by leading scholars and clerics to the global Muslim community which stated (in part), "Human activity is putting such a strain on the natural functions of the earth that the ability of the planet's ecosystems to sustain future generations can no longer be taken for granted."

Many other faith groups have taken a clear stance on the moral need to act on climate change. This includes many Protestant denominations as well as Jewish, Buddhist, and Baha'i organizations. CCL has compiled a comprehensive list of faith-based statements on climate change that is available on their website. Another valuable resource to explore is the Yale Forum on Religion and Ecology. Your individual faith community's website may also have links to climate change resources.

For Americans searching for a national interfaith group to work with, The Call to Conscience on Climate Disruption encourages people to express to their Congressional representatives the faith and morally based urgency for action. Similar to Citizens' Climate Lobby, a major goal of Call to Conscience's effort is to generate within Congress, official bipartisan recognition that climate disruption is real and caused by human activities, and is inflicting great harm on present and future generations and the Earth.

> *We believe that Congress will not act meaningfully – such as placing an acceptable price on carbon – until it recognizes the climate crisis. We seek to affirm the moral foundation for action, which an essential ingredient in the success of all social movements.*

Call to Conscience on Climate Disruption

Stand Your Ground

The knowledge that those of us calling for climate sanity are in prestigious company, standing on the firm ground of scientific consensus, is comforting and encouraging. Powerful as this is, though, grassroots support for the shift to a clean energy economy is essential. That's where you and I come into the picture. *Each* of us has a role to play in the coming transformation. Whether it's your voice, your energy and creativity, your financial support, or all of the above, this is an opportunity to make our lives count. It is an honour to be alive in times like these.

Time for Change Action Step

Commit the scientific consensus statement to memory:

> *97 percent of climate scientists agree, based on the evidence, that global warming is happening and it is human-caused.*

What's the best way for you to remember this statement? Write it down 10 times? Stick it on your fridge and read it every morning? Whatever it is, do it now.

Got it done? Great! Read and repeat whenever your memory needs a refresher.

This action step shouldn't take more than a few minutes, and will make a big difference in the climate conversations you are having. Your footing as a climate hero is getting firmer. Well done!

Good News for a Change

In August 2015 the Canadian Medical Association (CMA) voted to divest from fossil fuels. Citing the health impacts of fossil fuel burning in causing climate change and creating air pollution, the association will be moving its reserves of investments out of energy companies whose primary business is based on fossil fuels.

The motion was brought by Canadian Association of Physicians for the Environment (CAPE) board member, Dr. Courtney Howard.

"As a Northern doctor, working for action on climate-health is one of the most important things I can do for my patients," said Dr. Howard, also Northwest Territories representative to the CMA General Council meetings. "We are seeing respiratory effects from forest fire smoke, decreased stability of ice roads and changes in the availability of traditional foodstuffs. There is great stress associated with such rapid changes in the landscape. I am so happy that Canada's doctors have taken such clear steps to demonstrate to Canadians that climate change is a health issue that requires urgent action."

The CMA follows the lead of the British Medical Association (BMA), which voted in 2014 to end its investments in fossil fuel companies. The BMA was the first health organisation in the world to do so.

CHAPTER 6

Keep Calm and Price Carbon:
A Solution Big Enough for the Problem

> *Climate change activists and some politicians may talk about the need for fundamental change to avoid climate change, but the idea of a carbon tax has been oddly left out of the discourse. There is no policy instrument that is more transparent and administratively simple than a carbon tax.*

Shi-Ling Hsu, *The Case For a Carbon Tax*

During a bathroom break at a recent climate conference, my husband Mark had a sink-side encounter with an earnest environmentalist. This young Earth evangelist launched into a detailed description of the "greenest" way to dry one's hands. He shook his hands in the air 12 times and then demonstrated how one paper towel folded into quarters could be used to produce the required result. Like most people receiving unsolicited and unwanted advice, Mark couldn't get away fast enough.

Careful use of resources is an excellent idea for a whole slew of reasons, including the climate crisis. However, accosting strangers with random and uninvited suggestions for how they should change their personal habits gives environmentalists a bad name. Many of the global warming solutions offered to date have a similar focus on small-scale personal change. In contrast to the planetary-size of the problem, many of the suggested ways to address global warming have been individual ones such as switching to power-saving light bulbs and walking more. No wonder progress on this issue has been slow!

Don't misunderstand me; personal changes towards a low-carbon lifestyle are important for many reasons, and are part of the shift towards the sustainable future we all want. But the changes that your family and mine make aren't enough to decrease carbon dioxide emissions in a way that will change our current disastrous trajectory.

People are ready to hear big solutions for the big problem of global warming. When you break the meta-silence about the crisis and also discuss solutions, you are doing an immense service. Many people who are aware that global warming is a planetary-scale problem are desperate to hear that there is a solution comprehensive enough to tilt the scales away from disaster and towards recovery. That big solution is to make it more and more expensive to profit from polluting the atmosphere. It's called polluter-pay, and we do it at our landfills already when a "tipping" fee is collected for dumping garbage. The most democratic carbon pricing model is a revenue-neutral carbon fee. In this carbon pricing model, the money collected from polluters is evenly distributed to households to help us all transition to a clean energy economy.

Renewable energy technology is becoming dramatically cheaper and more accessible every month. The shift to a clean energy economy is inevitable; it's not a question of if, but how fast it will happen. A market-wide carbon price will accelerate the already swift pace of change. A steadily rising and transparent price on carbon pollution is the single best solution to our reliance on atmosphere-heating fossil fuels. It's a solution that is big enough for the huge scale of the problem.

As Tom Rand, Senior Advisor to maRS Cleantech Venture Group says, *"The market economy is the single most powerful social force in human history. Only a price on carbon can simultaneously harness the market to solve this problem, and at the same time unleash its creativity."*

Former Republican Congressman and founder of the Washington-based Energy and Enterprise Institution Bob Inglis describes a revenue-neutral carbon tax as good economic policy:

> *The practice of socializing costs while privatizing profit is not free enterprise. A prudent pro-growth solution is to shift taxes off of something we want more of, which is income, and on to something we want less of, which is pollution.*

Economics 101 supports putting a price on carbon. It teaches that what we want less of should be made *more* expensive; and the things we all want more of should be taxed *less*. Cigarettes are a good example of this principle; as cigarette taxes rose and it became more expensive to purchase them, the number of people who smoked decreased. Right now our tax system encourages what we don't want, pollution, and discourages what we do want, income. Taxing climate polluting habits and rewarding lower carbon habits is a simple and elegant solution for the climate crisis.

CCL volunteers lobby for a revenue-neutral carbon fee and dividend carbon pricing mechanism. Under a fee and dividend system, an annually-increasing fee is placed at the relatively few places that supply carbon-based fuels (the well, mine, or port of entry). All of the money collected is returned to citizens on an equitable basis. Under a revenue neutral carbon fee and dividend system, the majority of households will break even or receive more in their dividend cheques than they would pay for the increased cost of energy. This type of carbon pricing protects the poor and middle class.

A carbon fee doesn't have to be revenue-neutral to be effective. Government has a place in creating communities that support low-carbon lifestyles. Money collected from a carbon tax could go towards supporting public transit, expanding green spaces, and other sustainability initiatives. However, public trust in government is currently at an all-time low. Asking citizens to have confidence in government to make the best decision with a new and steadily increasing revenue source may be a stumbling block to public acceptance. Revenue-neutrality removes that hindrance. Once households start to receive climate-bonus cheques that both offset the increased cost of energy *and* assure them their government is serious about tackling climate change, the public is much more likely to embrace this policy.

Rather than using money from a carbon tax, projects for the common good could be financed by redirecting the money now spent on subsidizing dirty energy. A commitment was made in 2009 by the United States and Canada along with the rest of the G20 countries to stop the millions of tax payer dollars that flow into the fossil fuel industry's coffers every year. Despite this, subsidies to the industry that is destroying our climate continue. In 2013 the International Monetary Fund (IMF) estimated that global subsidies of fossil fuels totalled $1.2 trillion dollars. That's a lot of cash (2.5% of global GDP!) that should be available to subsidize industries and projects that don't destabilize our climate.

Like global warming, pricing carbon is a nonpartisan issue. Economists from all sides of the political spectrum are telling us that it's time to put a price on carbon pollution and recycle the revenues back into our economy.

Greg Mankiw, economic advisor to former President George W. Bush and Republican presidential candidate Mitt Romney, has detailed the conservative reason to support a carbon tax. Economists, Mankiw says, have long known that the key to smart environmental policy is aligning private incentives with true social costs and benefits. That means putting a price on carbon emissions, so households and firms will have good reason to reduce their use of fossil fuels and to develop alternative energy sources.

People are hungry to hear about solutions for the climate crisis. Too often the alarm is raised about climate change without at the same time providing a vision of the opportunities it provides. There are millions of jobs to be created and trillions of dollars to be made in the new energy economy. The opportunities available in the coming decades are so enormous they are hard to fathom from our current vantage point. Citizens' Climate Lobby provides a glimpse of the future that starts with putting a price on carbon:

> *By giving all of the carbon tax back to households - the end users- consumers will be able to pay the higher prices of goods and services caused by the higher price of fossil fuels. This allows businesses to pass along the increased cost and keep market share. Each year the carbon tax goes up, the dividend goes up as well. Everyone is on a level playing field for the first few years. But if businesses do not become more energy efficient and start converting to low-emissions energy, they will become less competitive and lose market share. These market forces will drive innovations in low-emissions technology, creating new business opportunities to develop, produce, install and service these products. This*

> *will create millions of new jobs here in America. American companies will be able to sell these technologies globally and American companies will become more efficient with the energy they use, making them more competitive worldwide.*

Think Local: North American Carbon Pricing

Here in North America, we're lucky to have examples of several different carbon pricing mechanisms. In 2008, the Canadian province of British Columbia became the first jurisdiction in North America to put a price on carbon. Starting at $10 per metric ton of carbon dioxide equivalent emissions (carbon dioxide equivalent, or "CO_2e", is used to describe different greenhouse gases in a common unit), the fee was raised every year until it reached its current rate of $30 per ton. B.C.'s current carbon price works out to just over six cents per liter of gasoline. Other fuels, like diesel, are also taxed according to their carbon content.

In a clever move, BC's carbon tax legislation included the provision that all of the money needed to be returned to taxpayers; the Minister of Finance loses 10% of his or her salary if this revenue neutrality isn't accomplished. BC's carbon tax now brings in more than $1 billion a year, and allows the province's middle class to enjoy the lowest income tax rates in Canada.

In 2012, California put an economy-wide price on

carbon by creating a carbon market, a carbon pricing system that is often called cap and trade. Two years later the Canadian province of Quebec joined this initiative, and in 2015 Ontario announced it would also participate. Cap and trade sets a limit (that's the cap) on the carbon output from large businesses. Businesses are then required to meet this limit by reducing emissions or purchasing emission credits (that's the trade).

Three years into the California cap and trade experience, the benefits are hard to document. However, during the first year of the program, the state moved from ninth to eighth largest economy in the world. California's GDP grew faster than the U.S. average, and its capped emissions decreased by four percent.

Cap and trade allows the financial industry to make money through brokering the carbon credits, packaging them into derivatives, and futures trading. Europe introduced the world's largest emissions trading scheme in 2005 with uneven results. Given Europe's lacklustre experience, and the lack of evidence to date that cap and trade can actually solve the problem of excessive carbon dioxide emissions, some scientists and environmentalists have expressed serious reservations about it. Despite this, China is moving ahead with a cap and trade scheme in 2016 that will cover 13% of the world's emissions.

Both ways of pricing carbon, cap and trade or a carbon

tax, can be effective in decreasing carbon emissions *if* they are designed to provide a strong economy-wide signal to switch to cleaner energy. The "cap" aspect of emissions trading provides more certainty about the amount of emissions reductions, and this is appealing. A carbon tax provides a more predictable price on emissions but, lacking a cap, may provide less certainty about the amount of emissions reductions (however a recent REMI study suggests a revenue-neutral carbon fee and dividend system would reduce U.S. emissions by 50 percent over 1990 levels in 20 years).

The attractiveness of a revenue-neutral carbon tax is its simplicity. Fee and dividend is easily implemented. It does not require a complicated trading scheme or on-going monitoring of individual industry emissions. An added benefit is that the money collected is kept in the mainstream economy and out of the hands of already-wealthy Wall Street bankers and traders. Cutting out the trading scheme also means there's less opportunity for manipulation and corruption, which has dogged the EU's program.

Get Excited and Price Carbon

The global energy market is the future. The solution to climate change is energy policy. And this market is poised to be the largest market the world has ever known. Between now and 2035, investment *in the energy sector is expected to reach nearly $17 trillion. That's more than the entire GDP of China and India combined.*

U.S. Secretary of State John Kerry

Never mind keeping calm, it's time to get really excited about putting a price on carbon! While it may feel strange at first to be enthusiastic about a carbon tax, the benefits of an effective price on carbon pollution are worth shouting from the rooftops. People want to get behind an idea or project that offers a vision of something better, not just hear a recitation of what's wrong with where we are now. When talking about global warming, make it clear that you are *for* what pricing carbon symbolizes. A clean energy economy and the clean air, water, and stable climate that it represents is something we can all get fired up about.

Two numbers that are vital for Ontarians to be aware of: 4, the number of degrees in this century that the planet is on track to warm, and 6, the number, in trillions of dollars of new economic growth that will result from moving to a low-carbon economy.

Glen Murray, Minister of the Environment and Climate, Ontario, Canada

Putting a price on carbon is all about creating a prosperous future. We have gotten to the brink of climate catastrophe because of the biggest market failure in history; the real cost of carbon has never been accounted for. Correcting this market failure requires a price on fossil fuels that accurately measures their *true* cost, in terms of health impacts, the pollution of our air, water and climate, and military expenditures to protect oil interests. An equitably distributed carbon dividend is the most honest and transparent solution to the need to shift our economy away from fossil fuels to clean energy. In doing so, we will create a better future for ourselves and others.

> *Too often the environmental left presents only the danger and not the opportunity of climate change... Of course it's a danger - the science is very clear. But it's also an incredible free-enterprise opportunity, because why do we have to be dependent on these stinky fuels? Why can't we have cleaner air? Why can't we have distributed energy systems that light up the world with more energy, more mobility, and more freedom? Why can't we?*

> Former Congressman Bob Inglis, Executive Director of Energy and Enterprise Institute

Time for Change Action Step

Share the good news: pricing carbon is a big solution to the big problem of global warming. It is imperative when you are having a conversation with someone about climate change to mention the opportunities that the climate crisis provides. Until recently the focus, for lots of good reasons, has been on the dangers global warming represents. As Naomi Klein has reminded us, the climate crisis changes *everything*. It is opening a window for us to create a society that values clean air, clean water, and our children's future. It is creating opportunities for entrepreneurs with a vision of a sustainable future; there's money to be made in creating that future.

Let people know that you are *for* something as a climate-concerned citizen. A price on carbon, and the shift it will facilitate to a clean energy economy is exciting. That economy represents cleaner air and water and a stable climate. Now that's worth getting worked up about!

More good news: no extra time in your busy schedule needs to be allotted when you take this step on the road to a stable climate, as you will already be speaking to at least one new person a day about this issue (if you need a refresher, see Chapter Two, step one). This step does come with a warning: once people hear what you have to say about the solution to the climate crisis, and the opportunities it represents, it may be hard to have a short conversation!

Good News for a Change

Georgetown, Texas has opted for renewable energy to save money, not the planet.

When municipal staff for this city of 50,000 examined their options, they discovered something that renewable energy was cheaper than non-renewable – in Texas! As a result, in early 2015, city officials finalised a deal with solar energy company SunEdison. By January 2017, all electricity within the city's service area will come from wind and solar power. "I'm probably the furthest thing from an Al Gore clone you could find," city manager Jim Briggs stated, "We didn't do this to save the world – we did this to get a competitive rate and reduce the risk for our consumers."

When Texas starts going green, you know that the shift to a clean energy economy is happening. There is no going back.

PART II
Unfrozen: Stories of Change

CHAPTER 7

Courage is Contagious

Throughout history, the really fundamental changes in societies have come about not from the dictates of government and the results of battles, but through vast numbers of people changing their minds, sometimes only a little bit.

Willis Harman, *Global Mind Change*

Courage is contagious. With that in mind, this section of the book is a compilation of personal accounts from people who have chosen hope and action over fear. Their lives have touched mine and inspired me on my climate journey. Their stories are shared here in the hope that they may do the same for you. I'm immensely grateful to each of them for allowing me to share their words with you.

We must do what we can. Always. At night we must go to sleep knowing that we have done our best, and that there is no more you can do than that. Do not let the problems overwhelm you. Start some-where, anywhere, with just the smallest gesture of compassion, and you have made a dent against the evil of the world.

Gottfried Müller, *The Prophet's Way: a Guide to Living in the Now*

CHAPTER 8

A Time Like No Other

John Price, a retired physician and a member of Citizens' Climate Lobby Australia, blogs about climate change and the future we are creating at grandkidzfuture.com. Here is John's climate story.

I used to practise medicine in Ipswich and teach at the University of Queensland, but now I'm retired. In 2005 Tim Flannery wrote *The Weathermakers*, a book on the climate problem. When I read it a while later, I began to understand that we live in a time like no other. I have a bunch of young grandchildren who will most likely live to see the last few years of this century. Long before then, as Tim showed, all our doubts and hesitations about the climate issue will be gone, and those kids will look back on our current behaviour with disbelief and probably disgust and resentment. They will know that if we had started on a fix for this problem when we first knew about it 30 years ago, we could have avoided most of its worst effects - but we didn't. And we seem certain to delay even more.

That's why I created the website grandkidzfuture.com. It wasn't long before the Copenhagen conference, and I thought if the delegates took a clear sense of the seriousness of their responsibility, this meeting might get the world started on what should be done. It didn't. In fact, you could take a very dim view of what happened there and say it's a sign that we'll never be organized enough. But that would be the same as giving up, and that's the one thing we can't do.

I've come to see that, although the climate problem is very serious indeed, it isn't really what has to be fixed. It's a consequence of something else - something about the path that human society has taken, especially over the last three centuries or so. The fact is, as René Dubos used to say,

> Man inhabits two worlds ...One is the natural world of plants and animals, of soils and airs and waters which preceded him by billions of years and of which he is a part. The other is the world of social institutions and artefacts he builds for himself, using his tools and engines, his science and his dreams to fashion an environment obedient to human purpose and direction.

Our imaginations, our creativity and inventiveness are such that we can make for ourselves civilized environments which are so compelling we can entirely forego residence in the first world - the ecological one - and devote ourselves to the many pursuits of the other; and that is what we have done, unaware of some very grave consequences accumulating fast during the latest century of our success.

So while it isn't too difficult to prescribe a remedy for the climate problem, it looks as if we won't be ready to take our medicine until we consent to something radical - changing our economic system to one that comprehends really sustainable ends. The age of cheap and plentiful energy persuaded us that economic activity could somehow grow for ever; but of course it can't. We only have to decide if we want that impossible dream to crash, or turn into something durable under our good care. That's why it's important we all understand what's happening and what's at stake - so we can make the better choice.

CHAPTER 9

Engineers Take on Climate Change

*Yannick Trottier and Vivian Grove Fulks are both en-
gineers who have committed themselves to acting on
climate change. While they share a profession, their
orientation to their climate work differs greatly. I have
learned from both of them. Here are their perspectives.*

An Engineer's Duty

Yannick Trottier, P. Eng, Citizens' Climate Lobby
Toronto

The reason why I act on climate is because I am an
engineer, and I made a commitment when I became
an engineer to hold the public welfare paramount.
According to engineer's codes of ethics everywhere, the
public safety should be the paramount consideration of

engineers in their actions.

Climate change is largely caused by burning fossil fuels on machines that were designed by engineering. In these circumstances when an engineer discovers that something that we have been working on causes potential harm to the public, we must report it to the client, and, if he fails to pay attention, to the regulators, and if they fail to pay attention, to the public, to warn them of the consequences of continuing to burn fossil fuels. This is a big reason why I have taken on the climate change cause and why I put so much effort into it.

Sacred Activism and Climate Change - Beauty Beyond My Wildest Dreams

Vivian Grove Fulks

The adage "Everything is Light" comes from the Standard Model of particle physics. Think of the recent Higgs boson "God Particle" discovery which suggests that everything is "aware". As an engineer and climate activist since 2007, I've tried to reconcile these theories toward what I call Divine intervention to our existential threat. In order to inform diverse thinking and beliefs, I compare religious mysticism with science to discover the interface. This interface is focused attention and is our collective definition of sacred. I travel to places where severe focused attention resides and therefore they are sacred sites- convents, cloisters, medieval churches, megaliths and sacred landscapes. The past focused attention makes these places sacred. I also started seriously mediating daily in 2009 which is focused attention on self and manifests as self-compassion. The more we focus on others, compassion arises which in turn makes them sacred.

The ultimate pointed focus of studying climate change is the mystery of death. The Creator to me is represented as the infinity symbol. We live at the intersection point of infinity during a speck in time.

Human evolution will require heroic compassion and emotional courage. We must evolve our compassion and emotions to survive because humankind is in the Anthropocene, or "the Age of Man" of the Sixth Extinction. Coral species are moving towards increased extinction risk most rapidly, while amphibians are, on average, the most threatened group. Mankind's and all mammal species statistical potential for extinction is fifteen percent.

Dark Matter is the glue that holds us together. **The glue that keeps us together (the good) is twice as strong as that which tries to tear us apart. Become the dark matter in your own world.**

Only five percent of the matter of the universe is visible and can be measured as planets or stars. The remainder is dark energy and dark matter because we cannot measure it. Therefore the scientists call it dark. It is dark because none of man's physical senses can see it, hear it, touch it but we can measure the mass of the whole universe and this dark matter and dark energy make up the other 95%. To me this describes the void that is the primordial life force. This is the Mother of all life, the Holy Spirit as created by the Creator and now discovered by science.

We have to create a new myth of connectedness where empathy and compassion for the least of these and where doing unto others as you would have them do unto you is rule one. And we have to start with planet Earth as being one of us. We cannot live without Her. We have to redefine what is sacred. Neil de Grasse Tyson's TV show remake of Carl Sagan's *Cosmos* is helping to do just that. Carl Sagan inspired a generation with his *Pale Blue Dot: A Vision of the Human Future in Space*:

> *Look again at that dot. That's here. That's home. That's us. On it everyone you love, everyone you know, everyone you ever heard of, every human being who ever was, lived out their lives. The aggregate of our joy and suffering, thousands of confident religions, ideologies, and economic doctrines, every hunter and forager, every hero and coward, every creator and destroyer of civilization, every king and peasant, every young couple in love, every mother and father, hopeful child, inventor*

and explorer, every teacher of morals, every corrupt politician, every 'superstar' every 'supreme leader', every saint and sinner in the history of our species lived there-on a mote of dust suspended in a sunbeam.

The Earth is a very small stage in a vast cosmic arena. Think of the endless cruelties visited by the inhabitants of one corner of this pixel on the scarcely distinguishable inhabitants of some other corner, how frequent their misunderstandings, how eager they are to kill one another, how fervent their hatreds. Think of the rivers of blood spilled by all those generals and emperors so that, in glory and triumph, they could become the momentary masters of a fraction of a dot.

...It has been said that astronomy is a humbling and character-building experience. There is perhaps no better demonstration of the folly of human conceits than this distant image of our tiny world. To me, it underscores our responsibility to deal more kindly with one another, and to preserve and cherish the pale blue dot, the only home we've ever known.

When the joy of compassionate service is combined with the pragmatic drive to transform all existing economic, social, and political institutions, a radical divine force is born: sacred activism.

CHAPTER 10

All That is Worth Saving

Alex Nicolson lives in Sydney Australia. He and his wife Rosey have been involved with Heart Politics over the years and have also worked with activist and Buddhist scholar Joanna Macy. They are part of Citizens' Climate Lobby Australia. Alex shared his story about why he engages in climate work during a recent CCL teleconference call. The silence that lingered after he finished was a testament to how moved we all were by Alex's words.

"My mountain is Mt Aspiring, named Tititea or Glistening Peak by the Maori.

My lake is Lake Wanaka, the name a corruption of Oanaka, the place of Anaka, an early Maori chief of this district.

My river is the Clutha River, named Mata-au by the Maori. This name referred to the river's swirling surface eddies.

My canoe was the MV Titan that arrived in Australasia in 1851 carrying English and Scottish settlers."

This introduction was the Maori practice as taught to us by John Broomfield, an expert on indigenous cultures and former head of the California institute of Integral Studies.

My ancestors arrived in New Zealand from Scotland and settled in the south in a city called Dunedin. This translates as Edinburgh of the south.

We spent all our holidays from when I was four years old at Lake Wanaka/Oanaka, a stunningly beautiful glacial lake some 27 miles long and edged by 6,000 foot hills. It is fed by two river systems coming off mountain glaciers, the Makarora and the Matukituki. The latter drains the slopes of Mt Aspiring/Tititea, the glistening peak. Lake Wanaka/Oanaka is drained by the Clutha River, Mata-au, which downstream is joined by two other large rivers draining adjacent glacial lakes before flowing eastward to the sea.

We boys lived in tents and ran through the tall pine trees and swam in the cold waters. As we grew we learned to fish for trout and salmon and tramp the rugged valleys and climb the steep hills. I took the beauty for granted and have always loved the outdoors and spend as much time there as I can.

Recently I trekked the Larapinta trail in arid central Australia on 1.6 billion-year-old rocks. This was a Yatra, or pilgrimage, a nine-day silent walking experience with meditation and reflection on self and the environment. One night we had a guest to our gathering around the fire, while the incredible southern hemisphere night sky moved slowly overhead. Jenny was an artist who had lived in nearby Alice Springs for 20 years. She led a conversation over two nights with the theme of beauty and damage. This conversation opened our eyes to what we couldn't see about the changes that had taken place even during her time there, the ongoing and cumulative impact of 200 years of western civilization on a fragile old continent and a 40,000-year-old culture of the original inhabitants, the Aboriginal people.

This summer I went back to New Zealand and stayed with my cousin at Wanaka. The beauty was the same and there were more conservation reserves. The population had increased a lot and the township was much larger. You have to be wealthy to buy a property there nowadays. Several ski fields have opened in the nearby mountains and Wanaka has become an all-year tourist attraction. Speed boats ply the lake.

Tumblr and Pinterest are full of photos of Lake Wanaka. Dozens of photos of the same scenes repeated over and over.

I savour the natural world. I observe that it is so majestic, so huge and old and also so fertile and re-creative of itself; in constant flux and regeneration and yet so timeless and unfathomable. It warrants slow perception over time. Great minds like Thoreau and Muir can inspire us, and old cultures with their connection and stewardship of the land and its spirit can guide us.

I think all that is worth saving.

CHAPTER 11

Hope in Uncertain Times

Teika Newton lives in northwestern Ontario. She has a Masters in Biochemistry, and describes herself as an environmental advocate. She is Executive Director of Transition Initiative Kenora and the mother of two school-aged children. Teika shared her story of hope on her Facebook wall recently, to encourage those around her who were feeling anxiety and despair.

Given the way the weekend went -having exactly the same conversation over and over again with every friend with whom I spoke - I think I need to pour my thoughts out here for the benefit of so many people I love and care about and who seem to be floundering and adrift, feeling alone, afraid, anxious and rudderless.

This weekend was the first really gloriously beautiful full spring/almost summer weekend of the year. I spent nearly the whole time at our new house, tackling some of the seemingly endless small tasks that are links in the long chain of eventually getting this project finished and getting us moved in at some point this summer. I took ample breaks to sit at the edge of the lake and watch clouds of thousands of minnows drifting along in the current, while the geese paired off through crazy, loud displays of mating prowess and virtue in the middle of the lake. It was so indescribably serene, peaceful, and grounding to spend this time fully immersed in my perfect little haven.

At the same time, I spent a lot of the weekend thinking about friends and loved ones all across this continent, especially my dearest girlfriends. There seems to be a common refrain – one that I heard from every woman I spoke with this weekend: we are living in really uncertain times, and often that uncertainty is frightening, alienating, or depressing.

Because of the work I do these days, I'm reconciled to riding the waves of uncertainty and it doesn't seem to be affecting me adversely as it is so many of my friends. I've accepted that my career is rife with uncertainty, from the direct, tangible level of not knowing quite how I'll be employed a few months from now, to the meta issues of the inherently unstable nature of climate change advocacy work (I mean, the climate is destabilizing... can't get much more uncertainty than that!). Rather than finding these times alarming, I find them thrilling and even delightful: the horizon is filled with endless possibility, and I am more hopeful now for a world that is beyond my wildest (happy) dreams than ever before.

At the same time, I recognize that in times of great uncertainty it can be hard to find one's path, and so many of my friends are asking the big life questions: Where am I headed? What is my purpose or mission in life? Where do I invest my energies?

Maybe this is just part of middle age. After all, most of my friends are around my age - in our mid to late 30s, early 40s. Maybe this is just the 2015 version of the midlife crisis. But it differs substantively from midlife crisis clichés of the 20th century, I think. Here, it's not a matter of narcissistically pursuing fading youth – the stereotypical driver of what I thought a midlife crisis to be when I was a kid. Rather, we are dealing with a clarion call to engage, to awaken, to connect, to become advocates and leaders and defenders of a world worth protecting. Also, I'm seeing this same urgent call to action striking my younger family members – women in their early 20s, through to my mom's friends in their late 50s and 60s. There seems to be a universal recognition that we're all being called to tackle the big life work, but for so many of my friends, this heightened sense of urgency is not illuminating just what that work should or could be. Instead, the urgency, coupled with uncertainty, just produces anxiety and even depression.

I wish I could offer up a one-size-fits all secret formula to finding peace in times of chaos, to figuring out how best to surf the waves rather than getting sucked down in the undertow, but I think each person does need to figure out the path that works best for him or herself, the path that resonates best with one's own integrity. Part of the current challenge is the intersectionality of all these complex issues: tackling social or environmental justice issues doesn't mean taking on a single issue in a vacuum, but rather attempting to effect comprehensive shifting of social norms. It's big work, and I guess that's why it seems so overwhelmingly huge and inscrutable to so many people. But the place to start is wherever you are, with whatever tools you have on hand, and to always remember that we are all in this together. We are not alone, and we are all interconnected in more ways that we can possibly fathom. Whatever small contribution each of us makes is one more piece to raising up the collective work done by all of humanity, and together many small pieces add up to massive, transformative movement.

Take time to be still. Be quiet. Listen. Breathe. Listen some more. Find the guidance of your heart by testing how different ideas or choices fit. Become mindful of the cues your body gives you: your body will guide you unerringly if you listen. If you consider a choice and it gives you a sinking feeling, a hollow emptiness inside, or it gnaws at your gut, for heaven's sake, choose differently! Find the course that leads you to feeling peaceful inside. Choose the direction that soothes and nourishes your soul, regardless of how unconventional, irrational, or downright strange that direction might seem when you imagine how others might see you. Don't pay attention to external judgments, including those masquerading as an inner voice of reason that challenges you to remain within socially acceptable conventions. Pay attention to how you feel inside, to what your instincts tell you, what you intuitively know to be honouring your own integrity. Doing this will not lead you astray; it just might lead you to marvelous new insights that will help transform the world into a more miraculously beautiful place than any of us can currently imagine.

CHAPTER 12

Renewing Energy

Kate Hale Wilson and Laura Sacks are both active Citizens' Climate Lobby volunteers who find inspiration through their love and connection with nature.

Breathing Deeply
Kate Hale Wilson

I love trees, the lives of trees as they cycle through seasons and span decades:

- the fire-bright shades of autumn (my favorite season)

- the bare-branched trees of winter: the fan of an elm, the gnarled meanderings of oaks, the slender grace of birches

- the subtle hues of emergent spring leaves

- the deep-greens of shady summer trees

I love standing beneath layered tree boughs, imagining the network of roots spreading beneath my feet. In the presence of trees, I grow calm. I breathe more deeply; my heart rate slows.

I am blessed to live among trees, in two green states— Wisconsin and Vermont.

I remember the terrible heat and drought of 1988, and how the leaves in Wisconsin's Chippewa Valley drooped and dimmed. I gave birth to my son that August; now I know that James Hansen testified to Congress that summer about climate change. I remember that Yellowstone National Park burned that summer.

I think of the trees of 1988 when I think about climate change. Sometimes I am haunted by the image of rolling Wisconsin hills or the Green Mountains in flames, and then my heart speeds up. Less immediately dramatic than these fiery images—but more deeply devastating— is the thought that shifting climate zones will destabilize forest biomes. Either way, something that I love deeply could be consumed—by the heat of fire, or by the gradually warming climate. So I breathe deep. I try to convert that fire to energy. I think of tree roots, and ground myself for the work.

Extraordinarily Ordinary

Laura Sacks

A special place for me is a mature forest on the shores of a broad section of river, where I regularly walk my dog. In some ways it is ordinary, as I go there through the seasons and the years, a place to let my dog run through the woods or swim for sticks – her favorite activity.

In other ways it is my spiritual retreat.

The light filtering through this forest gives the place an unreal atmosphere, where time seems to stand still. The textures and dark grays and browns of the upward growing cedars and firs contrast with the light green mossy understory. This moss covers years of decaying logs, where new life springs forth. The Earth underfoot is soft and spongy, smelling of moist dirt and fir nee-dles. A bald eagle calls in the distance from an island in the river, where a pair nest year after year.

Just off the trail are several large depressions in the forest floor, the remnants of pit houses from a culture which lived here perhaps thousands of years ago, back when these waters teemed with salmon. When I am alone in these woods, I often get an unexplained chill in the back of my neck walking in this area, as if I can feel the presence of another time.

And I am so deeply saddened that forest fires, disease,

and extended drought could destroy these majestic forests. On our current course, climate models expect this area to transition to grasslands by the end of the century. This place is just one of the reasons I am passionate that we must drastically reduce our carbon emissions. We can't let these dire forecasts become reality.

CHAPTER 13

I Couldn't Stop Now if I Tried

Sandy Aberdeen lives in Calgary, Alberta and is retired from work in quality assurance in manufacturing. He is a proud parent and grandparent as well as a talented musician. Sandy believes he must act on climate change because it is a moral and ethical issue. This is Sandy's story.

> *Every morning I awake torn between the desire to save the world and to savour it. This makes it hard to plan the day. But if we forget to savour it, what possible reason do we have to save it? In a way, savouring must come first.*

E.B. White, *NY Times*

In a way, we must savour first. Here is my story. I grew up in rural Ontario south of Ottawa. We lived on a gravel road with a few other homes around us. About a hundred yards behind our house was a wetland, what we called a swamp. I remember spending hours there as a child. It was particularly interesting in the spring. There were many birds flying around and perching on bulrushes. My favourite was the red-winged blackbird. The sound of the crickets and frogs could be quite loud at times and it was a challenge to try to distinguish the difference between the sounds they made.

My older sister showed me clusters of little black tadpole eggs and then we watched them develop. First tails appeared, and then they started swimming. Next they sprouted legs and then after a while their tails disappeared and they became frogs. It was magical!

Frogs are canaries in the environmental coal mine. Being amphibians they are more sensitive to pollution and climate change. Right now their numbers are declining at extinction rates.

One evening my parents suggested that my sister and I take a jar and catch fireflies. If we caught enough we would have a lantern, they told us. Fireflies only light up when they fly and they didn't have the room to fly in a jar. I think my parents knew that but my sister and I were kept busy for quite some time rounding them up!

There were no street lights or other lights around our house. I recall sitting with my family on our back porch looking at all the stars. Wow! So amazing and beautiful.

At the time I had no idea how lucky I was, growing up where I did. I have been savouring nature for a very long time and continue to do so. I couldn't stop now if I tried.

I would love my grandchildren and great grandchildren to experience the wonder of a healthy wetland as I did. It is my duty and privilege to try to do whatever I can to save the world so that future generations can savour it in all its beauty and splendour as well.

CHAPTER 14

Time Stood Still

Cathy Orlando is a scientist, educator and mother of three from Sudbury, Ontario. She founded the first Canadian chapter of Citizens' Climate Lobby.

Do you know where you were when you heard the conclusions of the fourth Report by Intergovernmental Panel on Climate Change (IPCC) on February 16, 2007? I do. I was in my living room. I worked from home at the time. It was lunch time. I was seven months pregnant and forty years old. The news came on CBC Radio. This is what I heard, "If humanity continues to stay on the same path of greenhouse gas production, the planet is going to be a very difficult place to live on forty years from now."

Have you ever been so frightened or shocked that your knees became so wobbly you could not stand up? That is what happened to me. I practically collapsed into my chair. I looked around. There was nutritious food on the table. I live in a city with over 300 lakes, thus plenty of fresh water. I have a great education, and I belong to the first demographic group of women who could truly follow any path they wanted. I was very healthy, forty years old, and pregnant with my third daughter.

What would life be like for my daughter when she was forty years old? Time stood still.

Extremely fearful thoughts of mass migrations of humans brought on by shortages of water and food as a result of climate change and consequent images of social disruption leading to war and its companion, rape, flashed through my mind. I saw all the women's rights gained in my lifetime dissolve.

Seconds later, I grabbed my very pregnant belly. I promised that little girl inside of me that mommy would do whatever she could to make sure her world would be Ok forty years from now.

Fast forward to September 2007; I was working from home. My baby girl was four months old. I was very sleep deprived at the time. I heard a report on CBC Radio that Mr. Al Gore was training people to give presentations on climate change. Immediately after I heard the report, I went online and applied to be a trainee. I come from a town of environmental heroes, Sudbury, Ontario. I did not expect to be selected. I don't remember what I wrote. They selected me. I think a combination of maternal hormones and a great education got me through the door.

I was trained by Mr. Gore and an incredible team of experts assembled by The Climate Project (now The Climate Reality Project) at the Climate Bootcamp on April 4-6, 2008 in Montreal.

A year later, at The Nashville Summit for Climate Reality Project presenters, I got to tell Mr. Gore my story. I thanked him for helping me keep the promise to my baby. He looked at me and he said, "Can I have a hug?" I said, "Yes!" What an honour. What a great hug.

PART III
The Summit is Waiting

CHAPTER 15

A Daring Adventure

The plain fact is that the planet does not need more successful people. But it does desperately need more peacemakers, healers, restorers, storytellers, and lovers of every kind. It needs people who live well in their places. It needs people of moral courage willing to join the fight to make the world habitable and humane. And these qualities have little to do with success as we have defined it.

David W. Orr, *Ecological Literacy: Educating Our Children for a Sustainable World*

Human beings are hard-wired to seek meaning. Researchers who explore what makes people happy have found a weak or nonexistent link between money and happiness. Rather, it's relationships with other people that impact life satisfaction ratings. Psychologist Dacher Keltner writes in *Born To Be Good: The Science of a Meaningful Life:*

> *This same literature reveals time and again that what makes us happy is the quality of our romantic bonds, the health of our families, the time we spend with good friends, the connections we feel to communities.*

What are we to make of the fact that in 2015 the wealthiest industrialized nation in the world, the United States of America, is also the most drug-dependent, incarcerated, and obese country in the history of the world? Out of the 26 wealthiest countries, the U.S. has the highest rate of youth homicides and suicides. If we believe the research, at the core of this societal unhappiness is a lack of meaning and connection.

It would be inaccurate to say that global warming is the sole cause of humanity's crisis in meaning. Rather than the root cause, it is a symptom of our disconnection with the Earth and with each other. However, the awareness, acknowledged or buried, that humans are racing towards self-created destruction is bad for our mental health. Humans are wired to avoid pain. That's good when it comes to pulling our hand away from a hot stove. In the case of climate change, though, that same impulse has kept us from facing the problem. Instead, we've stayed on the road to disaster. Collectively we've averted our eyes from the increasingly obvious warning signs.

Writer and activist Naomi Klein admits that for years she, like most of us, avoided taking a good long look at climate change.

> When fear...used to creep through my armor of climate change denial, I would do my utmost to stuff it away, change the channel, click past it. Now I try to feel it. It seems to me I owe it to my son, just as we all owe it to ourselves and one another.

The truth is that until we turn and face our worst fears, our ability to feel joy and happiness is decreased. The box in which we hide our fear keeps our joy from us as well. Humans aren't able to selectively numb emotions. When we numb painful emotions, we also numb positive ones.

The poet Kahlil Gibran wrote:

> Your joy is your sorrow unmasked.
> And the selfsame well from which your laughter rises was oftentimes filled with your tears.
> And how else can it be?
> The deeper that sorrow carves into your being, the more joy you can contain

A turning point in my relationship to fear came after I'd been blogging daily at 350orbust for several years. I had become obsessed with creating some security for myself and my loved ones in a world that seemed increasingly dangerous. Worry and fear were my constant companions. One morning my husband and I were having a familiar discussion about the best life decisions for our family. Until that day, these choices had been predominantly motivated by fear, trying to take into account all of the potential climate and economic upheavals ahead. Unexpectedly, I felt an inner shift occur. I realized that it was time to stop letting fear be the deciding factor in my life. For someone who had always been anxious, releasing that burden was a huge relief. My life on the outside doesn't look that different than it did three years ago, but my inner experience has changed dramatically. Fear still drops by regularly, but I no longer invite it inside to make itself at home.

The climate crisis is, among other things, an invitation to unfreeze our emotions. As Klein says, we owe it to ourselves and others to feel the fear; paradoxically, in doing so we will create the conditions to experience greater joy as well.

The Hero's Journey

Mythologist Joseph Campbell described the hero's journey as the story of a woman or man who, by persevering through a difficult ordeal, reaches her or his goal. Only then are they able to return to their community with gifts powerful enough to set their society free.

Whether or not you acknowledge it, each of us is on a hero's journey. A heroine faces the obstacles in her path by overcoming her fear, not by having none. Facing our fears is difficult, but not as difficult as a lifetime of hiding from them. If you have picked up this book because climate change is keeping you up at night, life may be inviting you to become part of the solution.

In her moving autobiography *Why Be Happy When You Can Be Normal?* Jeanette Winterson shares her search for her birth family after a childhood spent with a cruel adoptive mother. In the end, Winterson concludes that she feels lucky to be the fierce and courageous "me I have become" than the more conventional person she might have been without the craziness and pain of her upbringing.

Stories teach us, Winterson writes, that unexpected gifts are often found close to our wounds. The paradox is that only in facing our traumas can we unwrap those gifts. From Harry Potter to Gulliver to Christ, woundedness is central to the hero's story. While there is pain in the wound, there is also great value. Winterson recognizes that her adoptive mother was awful, but she has been able to discover the gifts that her upbringing has given her. She describes herself as lucky, and is able to write that, "she was a monster, but she was my monster."

Climate change is *our* monster, our society's ordeal. It's an invitation to each of us to stop running from the truth about our damaged relationship with the Earth and each other. It's a final clarion call to accept responsibility for the tab our industrialized economy has run up over the last centuries. Like every hero's journey, forgiveness has a place in this story, too. Once we've faced the climate monster, we can begin to forgive ourselves and past generations. We know better now, and it's time for us to do better.

Hope for the future is grounded in ordinary people like you and I being willing to take a step towards our fear. We don't have to conquer the whole "climb-it" mountain at once. We don't need to see the whole pathway before we take the first step; we just need to take it. And then another step, and one more after that. It may feel awkward at first, like working a muscle that hasn't been used in a while. It does get easier with practice.

Never doubt that we are not alone as we step forward to claim a better future for ourselves and our children. We stand on the shoulders of all those who walked similar paths before us; the civil rights advocates, the abolitionists, the suffragettes, and the millions of people around the world who, right now, are working for justice and the alleviation of suffering. This is noble and meaningful work.

"Climb-it" change is inviting us to choose life with a capital "L". Staying clear of danger at the foot of the climate mountain is no longer possible for any of us, but we can choose courage over fear. Helen Keller, who overcame overwhelming odds in her own life, wrote that "avoiding danger is no safer in the long run than outright exposure. Life is either a daring adventure, or nothing."

While the challenge of global warming may seem too daunting to take up, it is no longer something we can ignore. It's time face the fear that has us frozen and that is imperiling our children's future and our present happiness. We are frozen not because we care too little about future generations and the planet but because we care too much. This book's five steps up the "climb-it" mountain are an invitation to choose love over fear.

Each of these actions will move us all closer to the peak of the global warming mountain. At the summit is an awe-inspiring view of a new and finer world. That world includes cleaner air and water, along with a stable climate. It's a world where the health and happiness of our children is valued more than making a quick buck. It's a world teeming with marine life, flourishing forests, and humans living meaningful lives. The view from the summit reveals a place where democracy has been reclaimed, and decisions are made for the good of all, not just those with deep pockets.

The eyes of the future are looking back at us, waiting for us at the summit. It's time to accept their invitation and scale the climb-it mountain together.

The experience of awe is about finding your place in the larger scheme of things. It is about quieting the press of self-interest. It is about folding into social collectives. It is about feeling reverential toward participating in some expansive process that unites us all and that ennobles our life's endeavors.

Dacher Keltner

PART IV
Resources

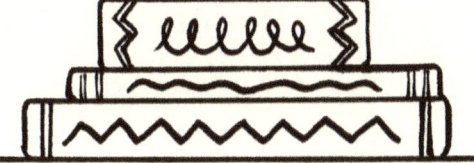

Where Are We Going and Why Are We in This Handbasket? *The Science*

*If you aren't alarmed about climate,
you aren't paying attention.*

David Roberts, *Grist magazine*

There's a bumper sticker that reads, "Where are we going, and why are we in this handbasket?" Its dark humour sums up what many of us know to be true. If you read this far, you know there are huge problems ahead for people and the planet. But how bad are things, really?

Global warming, it turns out, is only one of the most obvious symptoms of a huge planetary crisis that we humans and our industrialized economy have brought on with our misuse of nature. This chapter, which could have been titled "It's All Connected," will give a general overview of the state of the planet's vital signs: atmosphere, biodiversity, oceans, and global food security. There are many excellent resources available to anyone who wants to know more. A few of my favourites are listed in Appendix Three.

Some readers may feel too traumatized to read some or all of the next few pages. If you are one of these folks, take heart. The preceding chapters have highlighted steps that we all can take towards facing our climate trauma and fear. Some readers may always need to absorb this information slowly, one or two paragraphs at a time. You may need to take time for some deep breathing and walks, and that's okay too. Taking care of ourselves is part of taking care of the planet.

Global Climate Destabilization

Warming has also been observed specifically in the lower atmosphere and the upper oceans. Additional, indirect indications of warming include widespread reductions in glaciers and Arctic sea ice, rising sea levels, and changes in plant and animal species.

World Bank, *Turn Down the Heat*

Ninety-seven percent of climate scientists are convinced, based upon the evidence, that human-caused global warming is happening. Despite all the noise from the climate change deniers, the basic physics of our warming atmosphere has always been simple enough to be demonstrated in a high school physics lesson. There are naturally occurring gases such as carbon dioxide and methane in our atmosphere. These gases are natural, and have their place in regulating the atmosphere. They form a one kilometre deep blanket that allows us to live and breathe on our beautiful blue planet. But for two hundred years we've been digging up and burning long-buried carbon to fuel our ever-increasing number of machines. Oil, gas, and coal are ancient organisms made from carbon that have conveniently turned into fossil fuels during their time underneath the Earth's surface. These fuels powered the amazing transformation called the industrial revolution. But now we're stuck with underground carbon that has been transferred over the last two centuries into our atmosphere as carbon dioxide.

Those wanting to downplay the threat of global warming are fond of saying that the climate has always changed. No climate scientist anywhere would disagree with that statement. However, the reality is that our advanced human civilization has developed over the last 10,000 years during a time when the Earth's climate has been particularly stable. Over all that time, the average global temperature has stayed within a range of plus or minus one degree Celcius, year in and year out. We humans have been fortunate, and have taken advantage of our good fortune, particularly since the industrial revolution. We have flourished to the point that there are now seven billion people on Earth. To put this into perspective, it took all of human history to hit one billion people around the year 1800, whereas we've added an extra three billion in the last half century.

The same industrialized economy that allowed the human population to boom has poured heat-trapping carbon dioxide molecules into the Earth's atmosphere. We know that the average temperature of the Earth's surface increased about 0.8 degrees Celsius, or 1.4 degrees Fahrenheit, over the past century. Most of this warming, about 0.6 degrees Celsius, has occurred since 1980.

Human Fingerprints

There are ten main indicators of the impact our burning of coal, oil, and gas has on the global climate:

- More fossil fuel carbon in coral

- Nights warming faster than days

- 30 billion tonnes of carbon dioxide added to atmosphere every year

- Less oxygen in air

- Rising tropopause (boundary in the Earth's atmosphere between the troposphere and the stratosphere)

- Shrinking thermosphere (outermost layer of the atmosphere)

- Cooling stratosphere (second major layer of Earth's atmosphere, just above the troposphere and below the mesosphere)

- Less heat escaping into space
- More fossil fuel carbon in the air
- More heat returning to the Earth

At the 2009 UN Climate conference held in Copenhagen, an upper limit of two degrees Celsius of warming was officially adopted as the long-term global goal for greenhouse gas emission reductions. This goal remains unchanged despite repeated criticism from scientists, economists, and small island states. They would like the global goal to be below 1.5 degrees. The growing consensus among climate scientists is that two degrees of warming is too high to be safe, but too low to be possible.

> *The crux of the matter is no longer about the scientific validity of one temperature target over another... It is first and foremost about overcoming deeply entrenched divisions on value judgments, responsibility, and finance... It is about acknowledging that negative impacts of climate change under a 0.8°C temperature increase are already widespread, across the globe, and that danger, risk, and harm would be utterly unacceptable in a 2°C warmer world, largely for 'them' - the mollusks, and coral reefs, and the poor and marginalized populations...even if this danger hasn't quite hit home yet for 'us'.*

Dr. Petra Tschakert, Pennsylvania State University

What does too high to be safe mean? We have moved

from computer models to real world evidence of the impacts of 0.8°C global warming on our planet, right here and right now. There is increased flooding and drought, the Arctic ice cap is disappearing and glacier melting has been accelerated around the world. Global weather patterns are changing because of a slower jet stream, and ocean acidification and sea level rise are already occurring. According to NASA scientists "global climate change has already had observable effects on the environment. Glaciers have shrunk, ice on rivers and lakes is breaking up earlier, plant and animal ranges have shifted and trees are flowering sooner."

The consensus among scientists is that the world is currently on a trajectory of between four to six degrees Celsius of warming by the end of this century. With either one, we can be assured that the Earth will be inhospitable to human life in 80 years (give or take a decade or two either way). If we don't eliminate our carbon emissions, four to six degrees will just be a stop on the way to much higher global temperatures; hell on Earth, in other words.

The difference between two and four degrees is human civilization.

Professor John Schellnhuber, Potsdam Institute for Climate Impact Research

Climate Change's Evil Twin: Ocean Acidification

In pushing the climate and the oceans' geochemistry so hard and fast, we should also be wary of our own collective ignorance of how the climate system works. Perhaps negative-feedback mechanisms that we have not contemplated or have underestimated will kick in, sparing us debilitating consequences. On the other hand, little-understood or unanticipated positive feedbacks might make matters worse than we expect. We are humbled by a sense of ignorance.

Kerry Emanuel, *What We Know About Climate Change*

Not only has the global temperature climbed since the Industrial revolution, global oceans have become 30 percent more acidic. Scientists estimate that about 25 percent of the carbon dioxide pumped into the atmosphere every day is absorbed by the seas. What has only recently come to light is that when a whopping 22 million tons of carbon dioxide is mixed with ocean water every day, day in and day out, there is a cumulative large effect on the oceans. You and I wouldn't notice any difference in an ocean whose pH level has dropped 0.1 units. The same can't be said for many marine animals, particularly those at the lower end of the food chain. There is evidence that shell-forming animals such as scallops, oysters, shrimp, lobster, many planktonic organisms, and corals are already being affected by the change in the ocean's chemistry. Since 2010 Island Scallops on Vancouver Island has struggled to harvest their scallops before they die off from the too-acidic Pacific Ocean environment. In 2014, CBC news reported that since 2009 more than 10 million scallops had died before they were able to reach maturity.

"In 2010, we couldn't grow anything, everything died... Every batch we put through the hatchery either died at day 10 or by the end of its larval life, which is about day 20, they were all dead," Island Scallop's CEO Rob Saunders told CBC News.

Initially the deaths stumped those in the scallops industry. Island Scallops tested the ocean water for temperature and salinity, but not pH.

"I was trained at UBC, and we were trained that the ocean never changes," Saunders said. "It's the mother Earth, it's always stable and it hardly fluctuates, nobody was looking at pH..."

As well as taking the "shell" out of shellfish, the changing chemistry of the ocean is implicated in coral bleaching, a tragedy that anyone who has snorkeled or scuba-dived in the tropics will mourn. And, as mentioned earlier, more acidic water has impacts up the food chain. Populations of phytoplankton and zooplankton decrease, so that fish and many other sea creatures go hungry.

In summary, a more acidic ocean could wipe out entire species and hurt fisheries, tourism, and other ocean-dependent industries.

> *We confront an urgent choice. To move beyond fossil fuels or to risk turning the ocean into a sea of weeds.*
>
> Sigourney Weaver, Narrator, *Acid Test*

Biodiversity Loss

Biodiversity is defined as the existence of many different kinds of plants and animals in an environment. It is the variety of life at all levels of ecosystems, from the smallest to the largest. Throughout Earth's history the climate has always changed, and ecosystems and species have appeared and disappeared. The difference now is the speediness of the climate shift; *rapid* climate change affects the ability of ecosystems and species to adapt and so biodiversity loss increases dramatically. Palaeontologists call times when the Earth loses more than 75 percent of its species in a geologically short interval a "mass extinction" event. Many experts are saying that, based on the loss of species over the last several centuries and into today, the sixth mass extinction on Earth is currently underway.

The Center for Biological Diversity has stated that climate change is now one of the greatest global threats to biodiversity. According to the International Panel on Climate Change (IPCC), climate change will alter the structure and functioning of most ecosystems, will reduce biodiversity and will therefore compromise the ecosystem services required by all life on Earth.

> *Climate change will amplify existing risks and create new risks for natural and human systems. Risks are unevenly distributed and are generally greater for disadvantaged people and communities in countries at all levels of development. Increasing magnitudes of warming increase the likelihood of severe, pervasive and irreversible impacts for people, species and ecosystems. Continued high emissions would lead to mostly negative impacts for biodiversity, ecosystem services and economic development and amplify risks for livelihoods and for food and human security.*

Intergovernmental Panel on Climate Change,
Climate Change 2014: Synthesis Report

It should be noted that while climate change is exacerbating threats to biodiversity around the world, there are other longstanding practises that are also negatively impacting plant and animal species around the world. These include deforestation, which continues to increase around the world, overfishing, damaging agriculture practises, and pollution from pesticides and plastics. The good news is that addressing climate change will also decrease these damaging practises.

In summary, climate change isn't just bad news for humans; it is bad news for many of our furry, scaly, and feathered friends.

Food Security and Climate Change

One thing that humans of all ages, ethnicities, and economic status have in common is our daily need to eat. Without nourishing food we don't last long. But food is more than just a means of refueling ourselves. For millennia food has been a way to share and cement friendship and love. The joy of a good meal shared with family and friends can't be beat. And yet in the 21st Century, despite the fact that the world produces enough food to feed everyone if it was shared equally and used efficiently, millions of people go to bed hungry every night. The small farmers (who produce the majority of the world's food), are especially at risk of crop failure from changing weather, pests, armed conflict, and wildfires. There will be more of these events as the planet warms. The UN Food and Agriculture Organization (FAO) stated back in 2008 that the impacts of climate change were already being felt on the global food system:

> Food security is the outcome of food system processes all along the food chain. Climate change will affect food security through its impacts on all components of global, national and local food systems.

> Climate change is real, and its first impacts are already being felt. It will first affect the people and food systems that are already vulnerable, but over time the geographic distribution of risk and vulnerability is likely to shift. Certain livelihood groups need immediate support, but everybody is at risk.

Communities in developing countries tend to rely on agriculture as their main source of food and income. Subsistence farmers are particularly vulnerable to climate change, as it contributes to higher temperatures, greater variability in rainfall and greater frequency of extreme weather events, such as drought and flooding.

Although it is food-insecure farmers in poorer nations who have been first to feel the climate impacts, those of us in North America are not immune. As I write this, California is facing its fourth year of extreme drought. In January 2015 mandatory state-wide water restrictions were imposed for the first time in its history. What happens in California doesn't stay in California, though. The state produces 50 percent of the fruits, vegetables, and nuts consumed in the U.S. every year. In the Great White North, we import $5 billion of California produce annually, much of it during our Canadian winter. Thanks to California's drought, everyone's food is going to become more expensive, and affordable California strawberries and grapes in January may become a thing of the past.

Although not a food staple, those of you who appreciate California wine should take note that this industry, which contributes upwards of $25 billion a year to the state's economy, is at risk from drought and other climate change-related unstable weather patterns.

Climate Change is a Global Problem with Local Impacts

My ancestral lands are going to go through a 4 – 5 degree increase even if the world stays at 2 degrees...Grass stops growing at 38 degrees and our cattle will die. So whatever we have managed to preserve through genocide and colonization, we are going to lose through climate change. As an Indigenous person when I lose my land, I lose my culture. I am sorry about your recession. I am experiencing a bit of compassion fatigue. I am humiliated that I have to stand here and say how much, where, how? So I'm asking you for whatever your ancestors have done; if you want the climate fund be the restorative justice it is meant to be, can we do it now? Don't leave it for your children to share with mine.

South African delegate, COP 18, 2012

In summary, climate change is a global phenomenon whose effects are felt at a local level in a myriad of ways, most of them devastating. Those who have contributed least to pollution of our atmosphere - the global poor and our fellow species on land and in sea - are going to suffer first and most severely from a destabilized climate. None of us, though, will be immune.

Additional Resources

The following are some of the books and movies that I've turned to on my journey as a climate lobbyist. I offer them here if you are looking for information, insight, encouragement, and/or inspiration on your own journey.

BOOKS

- *Reclaiming Our Democracy: Healing the Break Between People and Government.*
  Sam Daley-Harris

- *A Climate For Change: Global Warming Facts For Faith-based Decisions.* Katherine Hayhoe and Andrew Farley

- *The Great Disruption: Why the Climate Crisis Will Bring on the End of Shopping and the Birth of a New World.* Paul Gilding

- *The Righteous Mind: Why Good People Are Divided By Religion and Politics*. Jonathan Haidt

- *The Hope: A Guide to Sacred Activism*. Andrew Harvey

- *Bury the Chains: Prophets and Rebels in the Fight to Free an Empire's Slaves*. Adam Hochschild

- *The Transition Handbook: From Oil Dependency to Local Resilience*. Rob Hopkins

- *The Case For a Carbon Tax: Getting Past Our Hang-Ups to Effective Climate Policy*. Shi-Ling Hsu

- *This Changes Everything: Capitalism Vs the Climate*. Naomi Klein

- *Animal, Vegetable, Miracle: A Year of Food Life*. Barbara Kingsolver

- *BUILD Prosperity: Energizing Manitoba's Local Economy*. Shaun Loney

- *Don't Even Think About It: Why Our Brains Are Wired to Ignore Climate Change*. George Marshall

- *The Energy of Slaves: Oil and the New Servitude*. Andrew Nikiforuk

- *Merchants of Doubt: How a Handful of Scientists Obscured the Truth on Issues From Tobacco Smoke to Global Warming*. Naomi Oreskes and Eric Conway

- *The Geography of Hope: A Tour of the World We Need.* Chris Turner

- *Active Hope: How to Face The Mess We're in Without Going Crazy.* Joanna Macy and Chris Johnstone

FILMS

- *Amazing Grace* (2006). An inspiring story about the abolitionist William Wilberforce and the movement to end slavery in Britain.

- *An Inconvenient Truth* (2006). The Noble-prize-winning documentary film about former Vice President Al Gore's work to bring global warming to the attention of the world.

- *I Am: The Shift is About to Hit the Fan* (2010). Engaging documentary by well-known director Tom Shadyac known for his goof-ball comedies like *Ace Ventura*. Prompted by a crisis in Shadyac's own life, the movie asks the questions: what's wrong with our world, and what can we do to make it better?

- *Lord of the Rings Trilogy.* It's easy to identify with Sam and Frodo's quest if you are a climate activist.

- *Who Killed the Electric Car?* (2006) and *The Revenge of the Electric Car* (2011). Surprisingly riveting documentaries about the demise of GM's EV-1 and, in *Revenge*, the rise of Tesla.

Notes

Introduction

1. Blake, William. "Gnomic Verses Me." *Selected Poems*.
    London: Penguin, 1996. Print.

2. Solnit, Rebecca. *Hope in the Dark: Untold Histories,
    Wild Possibilities*. New York: Nation, 2004. Print.

3. Klein, Naomi. *This Changes Everything: Capitalism vs. the
    Climate*. Alfred A Knopf Canada, 2014. Print.

4. "The 38 Best Quotes About Mountains, Climbing -
    Curated Quotes." *Curated Quotes*. 21 Feb. 2014. Web.
    5 Oct. 2015.

5. Seuss, Dr. *Oh, the Places You'll Go!* New York:
    Random House, 1990. Print.

Chapter 1. Hope is a Verb: My Story

1. "David Orr on The Paula Gordon Show." *David Orr on The Paula Gordon Show*. 20 Nov. 2009. Web. 5 Oct. 2015.

2. Thomas, Madeleine. "Climate Depression Is for Real. Just Ask a Scientist." *Grist*. 28 Oct. 2014. Web. 5 Oct. 2015.

3. Mandela, Nelson. qtd. in Morrow, David P. *Fat into the Fire*. Bloomington, IN: AuthorHouse, 2007. Print.

4. David, Korten. "We Are Hard-Wired to Care and Connect." *Common Dreams*. Yes! Magazine, 31 Aug. 2008. Web. 5 Oct. 2015.

5. "Nuclear Files: Key Issues: Nuclear Weapons: Cold War: Cuban Missile Crisis: Timeline." Nuclear Age Peace Foundation. Web. 5 Oct. 2015.

6. Shabecoff, Philip. "Global Warming Has Begun, Expert Tells Senate." *The New York Times*. The New York Times, 23 June 1988. Web. 5 Oct. 2015.

7. Thatcher, Margaret. "Speech at 2nd World Climate Conference." *Speech at 2nd World Climate Conference*. Margaret Thatcher Foundation, 6 Nov. 1990. Web. 5 Oct. 2015. (*used with permission*)

8. DiCaprio, Leonardo. "Global Warming 101." *Oprah.com*. The Oprah Winfrey Show, 27 Oct. 2005. Web. 5 Oct. 2015.

9.   "Vandana Shiva on the Problem with Genetically Modified Seeds | Moyers & Company | BillMoyers.com." *BillMoyers.com*. Moyers & Company, 13 July 2012. Web. 5 Oct. 2015.

- Gilding, P. *The Great Disruption: Why the climate crisis will bring on the end of shopping and the birth of a new world*. New York: Bloomsbury, 2011. Print.

Chapter 2. Talk Therapy: Changing the Climate Conversation

1.   Blakemore, Bill qtd.in Marshall, George. *Don't Even Think about It: Why Our Brains Are Wired to Ignore Climate Change*. New York: Bloomsbury, 2014. Print.

2.   Climate change and health. Fact Sheet. World Health Organization (2015, September 1). Retrieved October 5, 2015.

3.   Harris, Sam. *Reclaiming Our Democracy: Healing the Break between People and Government*. Philadelphia: Camino, 1994. Print.

4.   Rivka, Davia. "Climates Not Really My Thing" *Flying with the Geese*. 8 Sept. 2015. Web. 5 Oct. 2015.

5.   Tuscano, Peterson. "You Too Can Be an Effective Climate Change Communicator: 3 EZ Steps!" *Climate Stew RSS 092*. 14 June 2015. Web. 5 Oct. 2015.

6.   Kirk, Englehardt. *Talking Climate Top Climate Scientist Dr Katharine Hayhoe on Climate Change Communication Comments*. Talking Climate, 10 Nov. 2014. Web. 5 Oct. 2015.

7.   van der Linden SL, Leiserowitz AA, Feinberg GD, Maibach EW (2015) The Scientific Consensus on Climate Change as a Gateway Belief: Experimental Evidence. PLoS ONE 10(2): e0118489. doi:10.1371/journal.pone.0118489

8.   "Estimated % of Adults Who Think Global Warming Is Happening, 2014." *Yale Climate Opinion Maps*. - The Yale Project on Climate Change Communication, 2014. Web. 5 Oct. 2015.

9.   "Communicating on Climate: 13 Steps and Guiding Principles." *EcoAmerica.org*. EcoAmerica, 1 Sept. 2013. Web. 5 Oct. 2015.

10. Gilding, *The Great Disruption*, pg 9.

11. Duckworth, Angela Lee. "The Key to Success? Grit." *TED.com*. TED Talks Education, 1 Apr. 2013. Web. 5 Oct. 2015.

12. Ahmad, Omar. "Political Change with Pen and Paper." *TED.com*. TED2010, 1 Feb. 2010. Web. 5 Oct. 2015.

13. Kennedy, Robert F. "N.U.S.A.S. 'Day of Affirmation'" Speech June 6th, 1966." *Robert F. Kennedy Speeches : University of Cape Town.* rfksafilm.org, 6 June 1966. Web. 5 Oct. 2015.

14. Randall, Tom. "Fossil Fuels Just Lost the Race Against Renewables." *Bloomberg.com.* Bloomberg, 14 Apr. 2015. Web. 6 Oct. 2015.

CHAPTER 3. GROUP THERAPY: CONNECTING WITH OTHERS

1. Reynolds, Mark. Citizens' Climate Lobby Introductory Call. 7 May 2014.

2. Armstrong, Liz. E-mail interview. 22 May 2015.

3. "White Earth Wind Energy Graduates!" *www.whiteearth. com.* White Earth Nation Gaa-waabaabiganikaag, 15 June 2011. Web. 6 Oct. 2015.

4. Hadden Marsh, Amy. "Citizens' Climate Lobby Helps Citizens Take on Climate Change." *The Post Independent.* Citizen Telegram, 21 Aug. 2014. Web. 6 June 2015.

5. Anand, Y.P. "Mahatma Gandhi's Leadership – Moral And Spiritual Foundations." *Articles : On and By Gandhi.* Gandhian Institutes Bombay Sarvodaya Mandal & Gandhi Research Foundation. Web. 4 Apr. 2015.

6. King, Martin Luther. *Stride Toward Freedom: The Montgomery Story.* New York: Harper & Row, 1948. Print.

7. Harris, *Reclaiming Our Democracy*, pg 257

8. "What We Do." *350.org.* Web. 25 June 2015.

9. "May Boeve, Executive Director & Co-Founder, 350. org." *The Flaming Sword of Justice with Ben Wikler.* 25 Mar. 2013. Web. 18 June 2015.

10. McKibben, Bill. "The Great Carbon Bubble." *The Huffington Post.* TheHuffingtonPost.com, 7 Feb. 2012. Web. 30 Aug. 2015.

11. "Citizens' Climate Lobby - Political Will for a Livable World." *Citizens Climate Lobby.* Web. 14 Aug. 2015.

12. "About CCL - Citizens' Climate Lobby." *Citizens Climate Lobby.* Web. 29 Aug. 2015.

13. Wolfe, Craig. "Citizens Climate Lobby Lawrence Intro Session 1of4". Online Video Clip. *YouTube.* YouTube, 19, March. 2012. Web. 9 Sept. 2015

14. "24 Hours of Reality | Climate Reality." *24 Hours of Reality | Climate Reality.* Web. 6 Sept. 2015.

15. Ibid.

16. McKibben, Bill. "Do The Math." Do The Math Tour. Seattle, Washington. 7 Oct. 2012. Lecture.

17. Yong Kim, Jim. World Economic Forum. Davos, Switzerland. 23 Jan. 2014. Press Conference.

18. "Divestment From South Africa." *Wikipedia: The Free Encyclopedia*. 10 Aug. 2015. Wikimedia Foundation. Web. 24 Sept. 2015.

19. "What Is Fossil Fuel Divestment?" *GoFossilFree.org*. Web. 24 June 2015.

20. McKibben, "Do The Math" Tour.

21. Hopkins, Rob. *The Transition Companion: Making Your Community More Resilient in Uncertain times*. White River Junction: Chelsea Green Pub., 2011. Print.

22. "Transition Red Lake." *Transition Red Lake*. 2015. Web. 9 July 2015.

23. Hopkins, Rob. *The Transition Handbook: From Oil Dependency to Local Resilience*. Totnes: Green, 2008. Print.

24. *The Blue Dot Organizer Toolkit. Blue Dot*.The Blue Dot Movement, 9 Mar. 2015. Web. 30 Aug. 2015.

25. Global Oneness Project. "Drew Dellinger: Hieroglyphic Stairway". Online Video Clip. *YouTube*. YouTube, 18, Feb. 2008. Web. 6.Oct.2015.

26. "It's Time to Stop This Madness" Phillipines Plea at UN Climate Talks. Climate Home. Climate Change News. 11 Nov.2013. Web. 24 June 2015.

27. Shirkey, Robert. "Creating a New 'Normal': Using Air Pollution Labels on Gas Pumps as a Step to Addressing Climate Challenges." *OurHorizon.org*. Municipal World, Mar. 2015. Web. 6 Oct. 2015.

28. Jenkinson, C., A. Dickens, K. Jones, J. Thompson-Coon, S. Taylor, M. Rogers, C. Bambra, I. Lang, and S. Richards. "Is Volunteering a Public Health Intervention? A Systematic Review and Meta-analysis of the Health and Survival of Volunteers." *BMC Public Health*. BMC Public Health, 23 Aug. 2013. Web. 31 Aug. 2015.

29. "Volunteering to Help Others Could Lead to Better Health." American Psychological Association, 6 Sept. 2011. Web. 6 Oct. 2015.

30. Hawken, Paul. "Commencement: Healing or Stealing?" University of Portland Commencement Address 2009. Portland Oregon. 3 May. 2009. Lecture.

31. Kuo, Lily. "China Is Building a Great Wall of Trees to Fight Climate Change and the Encroaching Gobi Desert." *Qz.com*. Quartz, 27 Apr. 2015. Web. 31 Aug. 2015.

Chapter 4. Nature Therapy: Spend Time with your Mother

1. Dickenson, E. "Hope is the thing with feathers." *The Poems of Emily Dickinson*. Variorum ed. Cambridge, Mass. Harvard University Press, 1998. Print.

2. Louv, Richard. *Last Child in the Woods: Saving Our Children from Nature-deficit Disorder*. Chapel Hill: Algonquin of Chapel Hill, 2005. Print.

3. Louv, Richard. *The Nature Principle: Human Restoration and the End of Nature-deficit Disorder*. Chapel Hill: Algonquin of Chapel Hill, 2011. Print.

4. Jerpi, Laura. "Spending Time in Nature for Your Health - How Outdoor Activities Improve Wellbeing." *Spending Time in Nature for Your Health - How Outdoor Activities Improve Wellbeing*. South Source, 2010. Web. 30 Aug. 2015.

5. Lang, Susan S. "A Room with a View Helps Rural Children Deal with Life's Stresses, Cornell Researchers Report | Cornell Chronicle." *News.cornell.edu*. Cornell Chronicle, 24 Apr. 2003. Web. 7 Oct. 2015.

6. McBrien, N., I. Morgan, and D. Mutti. "What's Hot in Myopia Research-The 12th International Myopia: Optometry & Vision Science." *journals.lww.com*. American Academy of Optometry. Web. 7 Oct. 2015.

7. Kuo, Frances, and Andrea Taylor. "A Potential Natural Treatment for Attention-Deficit/Hyperactivity Disorder:

Evidence From a National Study." *American Journal of Public Health*. American Journal of Public Health 2004, 1 Sept. 2004. Web. 7 June 2015.

8. MacGregor, Catriona. *Partnering with Nature: The Wild Path to Reconnecting with the Earth*. New York: Atria Paperback, 2010. Print.

9. Whitecloud, Katherine qtd. in "World Religious Leaders: Bold Action Needed On Climate Change." *350 or Bust*. 23 June 2010. Web. 7 July 2015.

10. Standing Bear, Chief qtd. in Louv, *Last Child in the Woods*.

11. "Try Nature." *Nature Rx*. Dream Tree Film & Productions. Web. 7 Oct. 2015.

12. Kolk, Bessel A. *The Body Keeps the Score: Brain, Mind, and Body in the Healing of Trauma*. New York: Penguin, 2015. Print.

13. Macy, Joanna, and Molly Young Brown. *Coming Back to Life: The Updated Guide to the Work That Reconnects*. Gabriola Island: New Society, 2014. Print.

14. Aurelius, Marcus. "The Meditations." *The Internet Classics Archive | The Meditations by Marcus Aurelius*. Trans. George Long. The Internet Classics Archive. Web. 9 Oct. 2015.

15. Barrett, Kate, and Brian Hartman. "Foodies Celebrate White House Veggie Garden." *ABC News*. ABC News Network, 20 Mar. 2009. Web. 7 Oct. 2015.

Chapter 5. Science Matters: Know the Consensus

1. "Scientific Consensus: Earth's Climate Is Warming." *Climate Change: Vital Signs of the Planet*. NASA. Web. 10 July 2015.

2. "Methodology." *Methodology*. James Powell, 2014. Web. 7 Oct. 2015.

3. "Explaining Climate Change Science & Rebutting Global Warming Misinformation." *Skeptical Science*. Web. 7 July 2015.

4. Gettys, Travis. "Neil DeGrasse Tyson Tells Stephen Colbert That Science 'is True Whether You Believe in It or Not'." *Raw Story*. 11 Mar. 2014. Web. 8 July 2015.

5. Francis, Pope. *Laudato Si: On Care For Our Common Home*. Catholic Truth Society, 2015. Print.

6. "Islamic Declaration on Global Climate Change." *International Islamic Climate Change Symposium*. Islamic Relief Worldwide, 2015. Web. 8 July 2015.

7. "Faith-Based Statements on Climate Change." *CitizensClimateLobby.org*. Citizens' Climate Lobby, 1 June 2012. Web. 8 July 2015.

8. "Climate Change Statements from World Religions." *The Forum on Religion and Ecology at Yale*. Yale University. Web. 8 Oct. 2015.

9. "Call to Conscience on Climate Disruption." *FCNL*. Friends Committee on National Legislation, 2014. Web. 8 Oct. 2015.

10. Kilpatrick, Julia. "Canadian Medical Association Votes For Divestment and Reinvestment." *CleanEnergyCanada.org*. Clean Energy Canada, 26 Aug. 2015. Web. 8 Sept. 2015.

CHAPTER 6. KEEP CALM AND PRICE CARBON: A SOLUTION BIG ENOUGH FOR THE PROBLEM

1. Hsu, Shi-Ling. *The Case for a Carbon Tax: Getting Past Our Hang-Ups to Effective Climate Policy*. Washington: Island/Center for Resource Economics, 2011. Print. Pg 10.

2. Citizens' Climate Lobby. "Earth Too – Join The Mission." Online video clip. *YouTube*. YouTube. 16 April, 2015. Web. 10 Sept 2015.

3. Williams, Dave. "Carbon Tax on Front Burner for Electric Utilities." *BizJournals.com*. Atlanta Business Chronicle, 23 Nov. 2012. Web. 8 Sept. 2015.

4. "Tracking Progress: International Cooperation to Reform Fossil-Fuel Subsidies." *IISD.org*. Global Subsidies Initiative, 2015. Web. 8 Sept. 2015.

5. Mankiw, N.G. "Smart Taxes: An Invitation to Join the Pigou Club." Eastern Economic Journal, 35 (2009): 14-23. Print.

6. "Carbon Fee and Dividend - Citizens' Climate Lobby." *Citizens Climate Lobby*. 2015. Web. 8 Oct. 2015.

7. Brander, Matthew. "Greenhouse Gases, CO2, CO2e, and Carbon: What Do All These Terms Mean?" *Ecometrica*. 1 Apr. 2012. Web. 8 Oct. 2015.

8. "Section 1.2: Carbon Tax and Revenue Recycling." *Balanced Budget 2008 - Province of British Columbia*. Ministry of Finance, 19 Feb. 2008. Web. 8 Oct. 2015.

9. "Carbon Tax Report and Plan." *Province of British Columbia*. Ministry of Finance, 2013. Web. 8 Oct. 2015.

10. "Low Tax Rates." *Why Invest in BC Canada*. Trade and Invest British Columbia, 2015. Web. 8 Oct. 2015.

11. Hsia-Kiung, Katy. "From Sea to Shining Sea: Cap-and-trade Programs Showing Success on Both Coasts." *California Dream 2.0*. Environmental Defense Fund, 31 July 2015. Web. 8 Oct. 2015.

12. Nystrom, S and Patrick Luckow. *The Economic, Climate, Fiscal, Power, and Demographic Impact of National Fee-and-Dividend Carbon Tax*. Washington, D.C: Regional Economic Models, Inc. 2014. Web. 10 July.2015.

13. Kerry, John. "Remarks on Climate Change." *U.S. Department of State*. U.S. Department of State, 16 Feb. 2014. Web. 8 Oct. 2015.

14. Ministry of the Environment and Climate Change. *Ontario's Climate Change Discussion Paper*. Queen's Printer for Ontario. 2015. Web. 8 July 2015.

15. Holthaus, Eric. "The Conservative Case for Taxing Carbon Pollution and Cutting Your Income Tax." *Mother Jones*. Mother Jones, 16 May 2015. Web. 8 July 2015.

16. Dart, Tom. "Texas City Opts for 100% Renewable Energy - to save Cash, Not the Planet." *The Guardian*. The Guardian, 29 Mar. 2015. Web. 8 Oct. 2015.

PART II UNFROZEN: STORIES OF CHANGE

CHAPTER 7.COURAGE IS CONTAGIOUS

1. Harman, Willis W. *Global Mind Change the Promise of the 21st Century*. 2nd ed. Sausalito, CA: Institute of Noetic Sciences, 1998. Print.

2. Müller, Gottfried qtd. in Hartmann, Thom. *The Prophet's Way a Guide to Living in the Now*. Rochester: Inner Traditions, 2004. Print.

Chapter 8. A Time Like No Other

1. Ward, Barbara, and Rene Dubos. *Only One Earth: The Care and Maintenance of a Small Planet.* New York: W.W. Norton, 1972. Print.

Chapter 9. Engineers Take On Climate Change

1. Baillie, Jonathan E.M., C. Hilton-Taylor, and S.N. Stuart. 2004 *IUCN Red List of Threatened Species: A Global Species Assessment.* Gland: IUCN, 2004. Print.

2. Sagan, Carl. *Pale Blue Dot: A Vision of the Human Future in Space.* New York: Random House, 1994. Print.

Chapter 13. I Couldn't Stop Now if I Tried

1. Shenker, Israel. "E. B. White: Notes and Comment by Author." *NYTimes.* New York Times, 11 July 1969. Web. 9 Oct. 2015.

Chapter 15. A Daring Adventure

1. Orr, David. qtd in Stone, Michael K., ed. *Ecological Literacy: Educating Our Children for a Sustainable World.* San Francisco: Sierra Club ;, 2005. Print.

2. Keltner, Dacher. *Born to Be Good: The Science of a Meaningful Life.* New York: W.W. Norton, 2009. Print.

3. Krug EG, Dahlberg LL, Powell KE. "Childhood homicide, suicide, and firearm deaths: an international comparison." *World Health Stat Q. 1996;49:230-235.*

4. Klein, *This Changes Everything.*

5. Brown, C. Brene. *The Gifts of Imperfection: Let Go of Who You Think You're Supposed to Be and Embrace Who You Are.* Center City, Minn.: Hazelden, 2010. Print.

6. Gibran, Kahlil. *The Prophet.* New York: Knopf, 1952. Print.

7. Campbell, Joseph. *The Hero with a Thousand Faces.* First ed. Princeton: Princeton UP, 1972. Print.

8. Winterson, Jeanette. *Why Be Happy When You Could Be Normal?* Toronto: Alfred A. Knopf Canada, 2011. Print.

9. Keller, Helen. *The Open Door.* Garden City, N.Y.: Doubleday, 1957. Print.

10. Keltner, *Born To Be Good.*

APPENDIX 1. WHERE ARE WE GOING AND WHY ARE WE IN THIS HANDBASKET?

1. Roberts, David. "If You Aren't Alarmed about Climate, You Aren't Paying Attention." *Grist.org.* Grist Magazine, 10 Jan. 2013. Web. 13 July 2015.

2.   World Bank. 2012. Turn Down the Heat: Why a 4°C
      Warmer World Must Be Avoided. Washington, DC:
      World Bank. Web. 13 Feb. 2015.

3.   "Causes and Consequences of Climate Change."
      America's Climate Choices. Washington, D.C.:
      National Academies, 2011. Print.

4.   "Ten Indicators of a Warming World." *NOAA.gov*.
      National Oceanic and Atmospheric Administration.
      Web. 13 Feb. 2015.

5.   Tschakert, Petra. "1.5°C or 2°C: A Conduit's View from
      the Science-policy Interface at COP20 in Lima, Peru."
      *1.5°C or 2°C: A Conduit's View from the Science-policy
      Interface at COP20 in Lima, Peru*. BioMed Central, 27
      Mar. 2015. Web. 13 Feb. 2015.

6.   "Current and Future Climate Change Effects." *Climate
      Change: Vital Signs of the Planet*. NASA, 7 Oct. 2015.
      Web. 13 Oct. 2015.

7.   Schellnhuber, John. "Keynote Address." Four Degrees or
      More? Australia in a Hot World Conference. Melbourne,
      Australia. 12 July 2011. Lecture.

8.   Emanuel, Kerry A. *What We Know about Climate
      Change*. 2nd ed. Cambridge, MA: MIT, 2012. Print.

9.   News, CBC. "Acidic Ocean Deadly for Vancouver
      Island Scallop Industry - British Columbia - CBC
      News." *CBCnews*. CBC/Radio Canada, 26 Feb. 2014.
      Web. 13 Oct. 2015.

10. News, CBC. "Pacific Ocean Acid Levels Jeopardizing Marine Life - British Columbia - CBC News." *CBCnews*. CBC/Radio Canada, 17 July 2012. Web. 13 March. 2015.

11. "NRDC: Acid Test: The Global Challenge of Ocean Acidification." *NRDC: Acid Test: The Global Challenge of Ocean Acidification*. National Resource Defense Council, 17 Sept. 2009. Web. 13 Mar. 2015.

12. IPCC, 2014: *Climate Change 2014: Synthesis Report*. Contribution of Working Groups I, II and III to the Fifth Assessment Report of the Intergovernmental Panel on Climate Change [Core Writing Team, R.K. Pachauri and L.A. Meyer (eds.)]. IPCC, Geneva, Switzerland.

13. FAO, 2008: *Climate Change and Food Security: A Framework Document*. Rome: FOOD AND AGRICULTURE ORGANIZATION OF THE UNITED NATIONS, 2008. Print.

14. "California Agricultural Production Statistics." *CDFA STATISTICS*. California Department of Food and Agriculture, 2015. Web. 13 Oct. 2015.

15. COP 18, South African Delegate. qtd in. Kuusipalo, Rina. "Negotiating the International Climate Legacy - Harvard Political Review." *Harvard Political Review Negotiating the International Climate Legacy Comments*. Harvard Political Review, 7 Dec. 2012. Web. 13 July 2015.

Acknowledgements

It takes a village to complete a book project. I am grateful that my village included Valerie Blab, Suzanne Daigle, Catherine Mochrie, Kate Polle, and Emma Polle. This talented group of women graciously took the time to review my many rough drafts. Claire Cudahy and Lindsay Briscoe brought their professional editing skills to this project as well. Any errors are mine and not theirs.

To the gifted young artist Rebecca Saikkonen thank you (and your mom Carolyn!) for making time in your busy schedule to meet my crazy deadlines.

Thank you from the bottom of my heart to: Marshall Saunders and Mark Reynolds of Citizens' Climate Lobby for their inspired leadership; Elli Sparks and the CCL volunteers in the 2015 "Train the Trainer" course, for igniting the idea that led to *Unfreeze Yourself*; the lovely Linda Turner and Grace Cirocco, my ACEP angels who offered me guidance when I needed it most; and everyone who graciously allowed me to share their stories in these pages.

To all the tenacious people around the planet who are dedicating their creativity and passion to ensuring a livable world: *thank you, merci, and miigwiich.* You inspire me and give me hope.

For the last 14 years I have been fortunate to live in beautiful northern Ontario, in Treaty 3 country. I am continuously inspired by the land and the culture of the Original Peoples, the Anishinaabe, who have lived here since time before memory.

Above all I want to thank my husband Mark and my daughters Kate and Emma for what they bring to my life: *as you wish.*

www.ingramcontent.com/pod-product-compliance
Lightning Source LLC
Chambersburg PA
CBHW030315290526
45785CB00001B/375